MIRROR ON

1929

D1461862

ISBN: 9781790807659
© News Man 2018
All Rights Reserved

INDEX

INDEX - 2

INDEX - 3

INDEX - 4

POWERFUL NEW SERIAL BEGINS ON MONDAY

M. A. NOBLE
ON THE
TEST
MATCH

DailyMirror

THE DAILY PICTURE PAPER WITH THE LARGEST NET SALE

No. 7,841 | Registered at the G.P.O. as a Newspaper | WEDNESDAY, JANUARY 2, 1929 | One Penny

NEW
FREE
INSURANCE

HOUNDS ON CRICKET PITCH—NEW YEAR PROTEST GAME

Batsmen leaving the famous Bat and Ball Inn, where for years the "fathers of cricket" gathered after their matches.

Piccolo Jim on the cricket memorial. The local band played for the match.

The Hambledon (Hampshire) Hunt crossing the pitch on Broadhalfpenny Down during a cricket match played yesterday on a matting wicket between the Hampshire Eskimos and the Invalids, captained by Mr. J. C. Squire, the editor and poet. It was here that in 1750 was founded the first English cricket club. Yesterday's match, which was intended as a protest against the intrusion of football into the cricket season, was won by the Invalids by eleven runs.—("Daily Mirror" photographs.)

NEW SERIAL BY A MASTER OF MYSTERY ON MONDAY

LAUGH WITH THE PATER DAILY

DailyMirror

THE DAILY PICTURE PAPER WITH THE LARGEST NET SALE

No. 7,843 — Registered at the G.P.O. as a Newspaper — FRIDAY, JANUARY 4, 1929 — One Penny

INSURANCE PROTECTS WHOLE FAMILY

YORKS ROAD STOPPED BY SNOW

MARRIAGE OF THE LORD CHANCELLOR

Lord Hailsham, the Lord Chancellor, and his bride, the Hon. Mrs. Clive Lawrence, who were married yesterday in the Henry VII. Chapel at Westminster Abbey. Great precautions were taken to keep the time and place secret. See also page 24.

A motor-car stuck in snow on the road from Horton to Halton, Yorkshire. Drifts three feet high have been seen in places. Snow has also fallen in other parts of the North and in Scotland, where curling has been played.

BOOTS FOR MINER'S CHILDREN

CENTURY-MAKERS IN THE TEST MATCH

W. M. Woodfull.   D. Bradman.

W. M. Woodfull batted for Australia for four and a half hours yesterday in the Test match for his 107, and D. Bradman, who is twenty-one years old, made his 112, his first Test century, in four hours. Australia resume their second innings to-day with a lead of 327 runs and with two wickets in hand. Can England win?

The children of Mr. Joseph Guy, a Cannock Chase miner, being fitted with boots at Hednesford, Staffs. Mr. Guy is a widower and has an invalid mother.

REMARKABLE MYSTERY SERIAL BEGINS ON MONDAY

PRIZE MYSTERY STORY TO-DAY

DailyMirror

THE DAILY PICTURE PAPER WITH THE LARGEST NET SALE

No. 7,844   Registered at the G.P.O. as a Newspaper   SATURDAY, JANUARY 5, 1929   One Penny

COMPLETE FAMILY INSURANCE

MEN WHOSE TEST STAND SAVED THE SITUATION

Hobbs (wearing cap) and Sutcliffe, whose opening partnership of 105 in England's second innings against Australia yesterday turned a critical situation into one of promise.

Sutcliffe steps across to cut the ball, with Oldfield behind the wicket.

Hobbs playing a ball to leg against the Australians.

The stand made by Hobbs and Sutcliffe on a difficult wicket was one of the greatest of their Test match triumphs, and with the help of D. R. Jardine they left England with the task of making only 161 runs, with nine wickets in hand, to win the rubber and retain the Ashes. Thus, in a game which has been remarkable for its sudden changes of fortune, England has now a good chance of victory, especially as the wicket is said to have recovered and the weather seems set fair.

9

GIVE THE YOUNGER PLAYERS A CHANCE IN THE TESTS

GREAT NEW SERIAL TO-DAY

Daily Mirror
THE DAILY PICTURE PAPER WITH THE LARGEST NET SALE

No 7,845   Registered at the G.P.O as a Newspaper   MONDAY, JANUARY 7, 1929   One Penny

COMPLETE FAMILY INSURANCE

KING BECOMES DICTATOR

The Crown Prince of Yugo Slavia (fair-haired) with King Michael of Rumania.

GRAND DUKE DIES

King Alexander of Yugo-Slavia, who, faced by a political crisis, has suspended the Constitution of the country, dissolved the Chamber and assumed executive and legislative power. Existing laws remain in force unless suppressed or modified by the King, who has appointed a Cabinet to advise him.

The Grand Duke Nicholas of Russia, whose death from pneumonia at Antibes, on the Riviera, is announced. He was a cousin of the late Tsar.

MRS. PACE TO WED AGAIN?

Mrs. Pace, acquitted at Gloucester Assizes last July on a charge of murdering her husband, Harry Pace, is, the "Daily Mirror" understands, to marry again. She is at present seriously ill in Gloucester Infirmary after an operation. Also in picture is her daughter, Doris.

GREAT FLOODS IN ITALY—TIBER RISES TO HEIGHT OF 46 FT. AND ROME IS SERIOUSLY THREATENED

The waters of the Tiber nearly cover "the eyelet" in the Ponte Nomentano, Rome—a recognised index of serious flood. The river at Rome has reached a height of 46ft. and has caused widespread flooding, due to violent thunder, snow and hail storms. Parts of Rome will be under water if the river rises higher.

WILL PARLIAMENT SANCTION CHANNEL TUNNEL?

£1,000
PICTURE
PUZZLE
CONTEST

Daily Mirror

THE DAILY PICTURE PAPER WITH THE LARGEST NET SALE

No. 7,848   Registered at the G.P.O. as a Newspaper   THURSDAY, JANUARY 10, 1929   One Penny

LOMBARD
THE BEST
CITY GUIDE

PILED-UP WRECKAGE OF THE TRAIN SMASH

Pictures of the terrible railway collision, involving several deaths, between an L.M.S. express and a freight train in fog at Ashchurch, Glos. That above shows the overturned engine of the express with coaches piled upon it, and that below gives an idea of the damage done to the carriages and to the permanent way. Goods wagons were smashed to pieces and wheels and doors were hurled fifty yards through the force of the collision. The work of rescuing the injured, of whom there were many, and passengers trapped in the wreckage was performed amid a scene of fearful ruin and confusion. See also page 24.—("Daily Mirror" photographs.)

PICTURES OF BLIZZARD IN LONDON ON PAGES 14 AND 15

£500 HAIR DRESSING CONTEST

DailyMirror

THE DAILY PICTURE — PAPER WITH THE LARGEST NET SALE

No. 7,854   Registered at the G.P.O. as a Newspaper   THURSDAY, JANUARY 17, 1929   One Penny

1,066,237 NET DAILY SALE

FINISH OF 18,000-MILE FLIGHT

HELEN WILLS TO WED

Lady Bailey welcomed by two of her daughters on the completion yesterday of her 18,000 mile flight.

Miss Helen Wills, the lawn tennis champion, who is engaged to Mr. Frederick S. Moody, junior, a San Francisco broker.

Mrs. Wills, Mr. Moody and Miss Wills. This picture was taken at Wimbledon when the engagement was rumoured.

Lady Bailey's light aeroplane being pushed over snow-covered ground to the sheds at Croydon. In it she has flown alone to Capetown and back in over ten months and has passed in her journey over some of the trackless deserts and wild jungles of Africa and through storms and other dangers. She was escorted from Le Touquet, where she had been delayed by bad weather, by another aeroplane. On landing at Croydon she said, " I have enjoyed every minute of the flight."

THE DAILY MIRROR, Friday, January 18, 1929.

GENERAL BOOTH'S TEMPORARY SUCCESSOR: SEE P. 2

LAUGH WITH THE PATER DAILY

DailyMirror

THE DAILY PICTURE PAPER WITH THE LARGEST NET SALE

No. 7,855 — Registered at the G.P.O. as a Newspaper. — FRIDAY, JANUARY 18, 1929 — One Penny

£500 HAIR DRESSING CONTEST

BROKEN ROMANCE

Mr. Alfred Duggan, son of the Marchioness Curzon of Kedleston, and Miss Sylvia Jocelyn Nairn. Their engagement, announced in October, has been broken off. Miss Nairn is daughter of the former headmaster of the Merchant Taylors' School.

THE QUEEN'S CAR FOR A NURSE

Miss Eggie, district nurse, in the car presented by the Queen to Crathie (Aberdeenshire) Nursing Association. When the Royal Family were at Balmoral the Queen summoned Nurse Eggie to the Castle and, after talking of the nursing services and particularly of maternity and child welfare, considered that the use of a car, instead of a bicycle, would increase the efficiency of the work.

REMARKABLE STORY OF ABSENT DIRECTOR'S NOTE: "DON'T SAY A WORD AND SELL THE DOGS"

The house at Basildon, Essex, in which Mr. and Mrs. C. A. Brandreth lived.

The dogs they left behind and (inset) Mr. and Mrs. Brandreth.

No news had been received up to a late hour last night of Mr. and Mrs. C. A. Brandreth, directors of Ner-Sag, Ltd., mattress manufacturers. A gardener at their house told a remarkable story yesterday of a scribbled note from Folkestone, saying: "Don't say a word to a soul of removing furniture. Burn this and sell the dogs." Overseas Ner-Sag, a subsidiary concern, stated yesterday: "Investigations to date make it clear that Mr. Brandreth's estimates of profit and sales will not be reached."

PLEA OF A DYING EX-OFFICER: SEE PAGE 2

£1,000 PICTURE PUZZLE CONTEST

DailyMirror

THE DAILY PICTURE PAPER WITH THE LARGEST NET SALE

No. 7,861   Registered at the G.P.O. as a Newspaper.   FRIDAY, JANUARY 25, 1929   One Penny

LOMBARD THE BEST CITY GUIDE

TO DESIGN THE HAIG MEMORIAL   THE QUEEN OPENS HOME FOR NURSES

Mr. W. McMillan, A.R.A., with cast for a memorial.

Mr. Gilbert Ledward with model of Guards' Memorial.

Two of the three distinguished sculptors who have been invited by the Government to submit designs for the bronze equestrian statue of Earl Haig, which is to be erected in Whitehall as a memorial to Britain's chief commander in the Great War. It will stand opposite the Scottish Office.

The Queen leaving after performing the ceremony.

A large crowd welcoming the Queen on her arrival to lay the foundation stone of a nurses' home for Middlesex Hospital. The home, which will cost £200,000, is the gift of an anonymous donor, whose name, in a sealed envelope, was placed beneath the stone.

This was the Queen's first appearance at a public function since the news of the King's progress towards recovery was published. A seventeenth-century barber-surgeon's bowl was presented to her as a memento of the visit.

THE DAILY MIRROR, Tuesday, January 29, 1929.

WOMEN'S VOTES: FIRST RESULTS OF OUR BALLOT

MORE INSURANCE CLAIMS PAID

DailyMirror

THE DAILY PICTURE PAPER WITH THE LARGEST NET SALE

No. 7,864 — Registered at the G.P.O. as a Newspaper. — TUESDAY, JANUARY 29, 1929 — One Penny

£100 CROSSWORD TO-DAY

FIRST PICTURES OF THE AFGHAN CIVIL WAR

Aeroplanes standing on the snow-covered aerodrome outside Kabul waiting for the European women and children whom they carried to safety at Peshawar, India.

The rebels of Bachai Sachao made the clock tower a frequent target.

A shell hole in the wall and a shattered window at the British Legation.

The Union Jack above the shot-marked walls of the British Legation.

Remains of the Military Attache's house, which took fire during the shelling.

These exclusive " Daily Mirror " photographs are the first to reach London illustrating the fighting round the British Legation at Kabul and the rescue of European women and children from their perilous position in the Afghan capital. The situation there is now even more precarious, and at any moment it may be necessary to bring away Sir

Francis Humphrys, the British Minister, and other European men. The reign of Bachai Sachao, the brigand, who has made himself Amir, is not expected to last long, and it was reported yesterday that Amanullah has " reaccepted the reins of government " at the request of the people of Kandahar.

THE DAILY MIRROR, Thursday, January 31, 1929.

WHAT WILL HAPPEN TO GODDARD'S £12,000? See p. 17

£1,000 PICTURE PUZZLE CONTEST

DailyMirror

THE DAILY PICTURE PAPER WITH THE LARGEST NET SALE

No. 7,866   Registered at the G.P.O. as a Newspaper.   THURSDAY, JANUARY 31, 1929   One Penny

INSURANCE PROTECTS WHOLE FAMILY

THE PRINCE APPALLED BY MINERS' DISTRESS

The Prince of Wales leaving a miner's home in Wapping Square, a hamlet near Newcastle, during his tour yesterday of the distressed areas in the Northumberland coal district.

PASSENGERS' ESCAPE IN TRAIN MISHAP

The engine of a boat train from Harwich to Liverpool-street overturned near Wrabness, Essex, in passing goods trucks which had been derailed. Two mail vans of the boat train were also derailed, but no one was seriously hurt.

Cottages of Wapping Square. In one the Prince was shocked to find a family of eight living in two rooms with no beds. "Isn't it ghastly!" he remarked. The cottage which the Prince is seen leaving in the picture above is by the lamp-post.

16

WHERE IS COL. RUTHERFORD?—CANADA MYSTERY

PRIZE MYSTERY STORY TO-DAY

DailyMirror

THE DAILY PICTURE PAPER WITH THE LARGEST NET SALE

No. 7,868 Registered at the G.P.O. as a Newspaper. SATURDAY, FEBRUARY 2, 1929 One Penny

£1,000 CONTEST EVERY WEEK

MISSING LONDON GIRLS

Rose O'Grady, aged twenty-three. Muriel Dunsmuir, aged eleven.

Muriel Dunsmuir and Rose O'Grady, a maid, who are missing from the hotel at Putney at which Mrs. Dunsmuir has been staying with her children. It is suggested that they may have gone to Ireland, where Miss O'Grady's parents live, and that they may try to appear together on the stage. Mrs. Dunsmuir's husband, who died three weeks ago, was at one time Lieutenant-Governor of British Columbia.

GUARD FOR THE KING

Men from the royal yacht Victoria and Albert, building a shelter for the guard which is to be stationed at the entrance to Craigweil House, near Bognor, during the King's stay. In view of the satisfactory progress which the King continues to make, the doctors will issue no bulletin until Monday.—("Daily Mirror" photograph.)

MAIL BAG STOLEN FROM VAN IN LONDON STREET

Detectives conducting investigations at Mount Pleasant sorting office yesterday into the huge mail bag robbery. A bag containing parcels addressed, it is believed, to jewellers, a bank and a Hatton-garden firm was missed from a van passing through the City. It is said that diamonds were in one of the parcels.

PROMOTION

Chief Inspector Cornish, of Scotland Yard, whose promotion to the rank of superintendent was announced last night. He has figured in some of the most famous of recent criminal cases.

£1,600 AWARD

Miss M. Nicol, a Government typist, who yesterday was awarded £1,600 damages in her breach of promise action against Mr. Ernest Boond, an Air Ministry accountant.

THE DAILY MIRROR, Wednesday, February 6, 1929.

BOMBAY RIOTS: BRITISH TROOPS CALLED OUT

WOMEN'S VOTES: MORE FIGURES

DailyMirror

THE DAILY PICTURE PAPER WITH THE LARGEST NET SALE

No. 7,871 — Registered at the G.P.O. as a Newspaper. — WEDNESDAY, FEBRUARY 6, 1929 — One Penny

£1,000 CONTEST EVERY WEEK

FOR BETTER AND BIGGER EGGS

ROCKET SLEIGH

Herr Max Valier and his wife kissing before their trials, which were on the frozen Lake Eibse.

Mr. Walter Guinness, Minister of Agriculture, manipulating the machine with which eggs are weighed and graded at the national egg-packing station which he opened yesterday at Hungerford, Berks. Next to him is Viscount Folkestone (X).—("Daily Mirror.")

BACK IN LONDON

Muriel Dunsmuir at Paddington yesterday on return with her mother from Ireland. At South-Western Police Court, Rose O'Grady was remanded in custody on a charge of abducting the child.

Herr Max Valier's rocket sleigh during a successful trial in the Bavarian Alps. His wife was at the wheel. Later a speed of over sixty miles an hour was reached. A rocket car designed by Herr Valier was destroyed during a trial run last year.—(Exclusive photographs.)

THE DAILY MIRROR, Thursday, February 7, 1929.

BATON CHARGES BY POLICE IN PITHEAD CLASH

£1,000
CONTEST
EVERY
WEEK

Daily Mirror

THE DAILY PICTURE PAPER WITH THE LARGEST NET SALE

COMPLETE
FAMILY
INSURANCE

No. 7,872   Registered at the G.P.O. as a Newspaper.   THURSDAY, FEBRUARY 7, 1929   One Penny

THE DUCHESS AT HER BROTHER'S WEDDING

The Duchess of York with the Duke leaving after her brother's wedding yesterday.

The bride and bridegroom walking to their carriage after the ceremony.

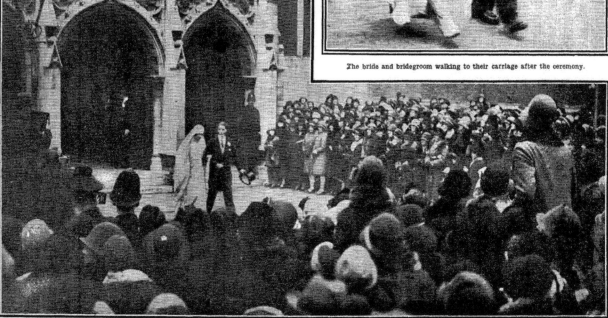

The crowd round the church door watching the bride and bridegroom depart. Many people had waited for four hours, and hundreds were kept at a distance by police.

The Duchess of York was a central figure among the guests at the wedding at St. Margaret's, Westminster, yesterday of her youngest brother, the Hon. David Bowes-Lyon, and Miss Rachel Spender-Clay, daughter of Lt.-Col. H. H. Spender-Clay, M.P., and a niece of Viscount Astor. The ceremony was performed by Lord Davidson, formerly Archbishop of Canterbury. The bride wore a medieval gown of gold-tinted brocade with a veil of old lace, and a skirt which reached the ground.

BEST FAMILY INSURANCE: REGISTER TO-DAY

LOMBARD THE BEST CITY GUIDE

DailyMirror

THE DAILY PICTURE PAPER WITH THE LARGEST NET SALE

No. 7,875 | Registered at the G.P.O. as a Newspaper. | MONDAY, FEBRUARY 11, 1929 | One Penny

NEW £1,000 CONTEST TO-DAY

5 PASSENGERS HURT IN TRAIN MISHAP AT STOKE

Five passengers were hurt in a train accident near Stoke-on-Trent yesterday. See page 3.—(Picture by the " Daily Mirror " photo-telephony system.)

THE KING'S JOURNEY BY AMBULANCE TO BOGNOR FOR HIS CONVALESCENCE

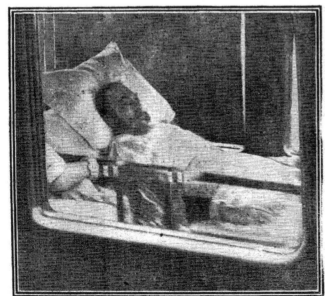

The King in the ambulance during his journey from Buckingham Palace to Bognor.

Nurse Black accompanying the King in his ambulance.

The Queen arriving at Bognor half an hour before the King.

His Majesty waves his handkerchief to the people as he passes.

After a very good night, following his journey to Bognor, Sussex, the King yesterday was said to have benefited already by the change of air and surroundings. He was carried from his room at the Palace to the ambulance by four ambulance men. He joked with them, and during his journey waved to the crowds.

20

THE DAILY MIRROR. Thursday, February 14, 1929

BRITAIN'S ARCTIC WEATHER TO CONTINUE

NEW SERIAL ON MONDAY

Daily Mirror

THE DAILY PICTURE PAPER WITH THE LARGEST NET SALE

No 7,878   Registered at the G.P.O. as a Newspaper.   THURSDAY, FEBRUARY 14, 1929   One Penny

£1,000 RACING CONTEST COUPON TO-DAY

THE POPE, NOW A SOVEREIGN, BLESSES ROME

ope Pius XI. (x) blessing the populace of Rome assembled before St. Peter's Cathedral after the reconciliation between the Papacy and the Italian Government.

The huge Roman crowd standing under umbrellas in the Piazza San Pietro to receive the blessing of His Holiness the Pope from the balcony of St. Peter's (marked x). There was the utmost enthusiasm throughout the city. Government offices were decorated with flags, the yellow and white colours of the Holy See appearing side by side with the green, white and red tricolour of Italy. Many Papal flags were also flown at private houses.—("Daily Mirror" exclusive photographs.)

BRILLIANT NEW SERIAL ON MONDAY NEXT

COMPLETE FAMILY INSURANCE

Daily Mirror

THE DAILY PICTURE PAPER WITH THE LARGEST NET SALE

No. 7,879   Registered at the G.P.O. as a Newspaper.   FRIDAY, FEBRUARY 15, 1929   One Penny

£1,000 PRIZE EVERY WEEK

THE SEVEREST FROSTBITE OF THE WINTER

Shovelling a way along a part of the road between Abergavenny and Merthyr Tydfil, South Wales, which was rendered impassable in many places by a deep snowdrift.

A frozen pump by the River Lea at Clapton. Six inches of ice had to be broken off with hammer blows.

People walking on the frozen river at Dordrecht, in South Holland. Paths have been made across the ice.

The lock-keeper at Molesey, Surrey, passing masses of floating ice through the lock.

This year's severest frostbite was experienced yesterday at Ross-on-Wye (Herefordshire), where forty degrees of frost was registered. In many other places the temperature was little higher. The Thames was nearly frozen over in some parts; a hot spring at Matlock (Derbyshire) froze; football was played on the River Nen at Northampton; skating was being enjoyed everywhere, and two engines on a Scottish express became frostbound and had to be replaced. See also pages 14 and 15.

22

£1,000 RACING CONTEST: COUPON TO-DAY

ANOTHER PRIZE MYSTERY STORY

DailyMirror
THE DAILY PICTURE ● PAPER WITH THE LARGEST NET SALE

NEW SERIAL ON MONDAY

No. 7,880 | Registered at the G.P.O. as a Newspaper. | SATURDAY, FEBRUARY 16, 1929 | One Penny

WARSHIPS CUT PASSAGE TO ICEBOUND VESSELS

The German battleship Elsass breaking her way through the frozen Western Baltic to free ships imprisoned by the ice.

Snowed up in a country lane—a common sight these days

The Thames frozen over at Molesey (Surrey) yesterday.

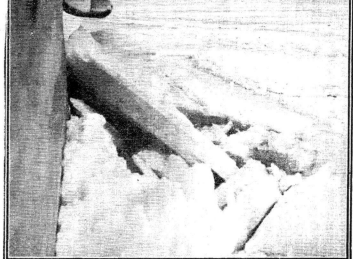

The powerful bows of the German battleship, Schleswig-Holstein, cutting an easy passage through ice.

German warships have been engaged for days in rescuing some of the hundreds of vessels which have been icebound in the Baltic, and where they have failed to force a passage provisions have been sent to the stranded sailors and passengers by aeroplane or sledges.

In Britain the frost continued yesterday as keen as ever and last night it was officially stated that falls of snow might be expected. No anticipation of a thaw was revealed. Further cold weather pictures are on pages 12 and 13.

THE DAILY MIRROR, Tuesday, February 19, 1929.

BEGIN OUR BRILLIANT NEW SERIAL TO-DAY: P. 17

WOMEN'S VOTES: LATEST FIGURES

DailyMirror

THE DAILY PICTURE PAPER WITH THE LARGEST NET SALE

No. 7,882 | Registered at the G.P.O. as a Newspaper. | TUESDAY, FEBRUARY 19, 1929 | One Penny

MORE INSURANCE CLAIMS PAID

FIRST SKATING ON THAMES FOR 34 YEARS

Skating on the frozen Thames between Medley and Godstow, the first time such a thing has been known for thirty-four years. Those who hoped for a thaw yesterday have been disappointed.

IN THE NEWS

Miss H. T. Tetley, of Chalfont St. Giles (Bucks) who, in the High Court yesterday, said she had lost £9,000 in financing a speculation on the advice of a neighbour and friend. Her action was settled.

Miss Marie King, aged twenty-six, a golfer, of Clacton, found dead with her head in a gas oven by her mother on returning from skating.

PRINCE OF WALES AT BRITISH INDUSTRIES FAIR DINNER

The scene at the banquet last night of the British Industries Fair, held at the Mansion House. In the smaller picture is the Prince of Wales photographed at this function. It was his first public dinner since the illness of the King, and there were also present the Prime Minister, Mr. Baldwin, and the American Ambassador, Mr. A. B. Houghton. Pictures of the Fair are on page 28.

THE DAILY MIRROR, Friday, February 22, 1929.

STRANGE RIDDLE OF GIRL FOUND DEAD IN FIELD

LOMBARD
THE BEST
CITY GUIDE

DailyMirror

THE DAILY PICTURE PAPER WITH THE LARGEST NET SALE

No. 7,885 Registered at the G.P.O. as a Newspaper. FRIDAY, FEBRUARY 22, 1929 One Penny

£1,000
PRIZE
EVERY
WEEK

THAW DRAMA

Wilfred Archer, killed yesterday at a Nottingham colliery by an accident due to the thaw, with his wife.

The shaft-head at the Bestwood Colliery, where the accident occurred, and (inset) Percy Davy, who was also killed. As the cage containing fourteen men was ascending the shaft, a mass of ice, dislodged by the thaw, and some masonry crashed into its upper deck. Three other men suffered broken arms.

SEA GIANT OUT OF WATER

The world's biggest ship, the White Star liner Majestic, of 56,000 tons, inside the world's largest floating dock, of 60,000 tons, which she entered yesterday at Southampton for overhaul. She will be high and dry for two weeks.

THE DUKE AND BRITISH TRADE

The Duke of York watching a demonstration of a new drill at the Birmingham section of the British Industries Fair yesterday. He was loudly cheered as he drove through the streets.—(" Daily Mirror " photograph.)

The huge propellers of the Majestic above the dock floor.—" Daily Mirror " photographs.)

DUTCH STORY OF FRANCO-BELGIAN MILITARY PACT

RACING
CONTEST
COUPON
TO-DAY

Daily Mirror

THE DAILY PICTURE PAPER WITH THE LARGEST NET SALE

NEW
£1,000
PICTURE
PUZZLE

No. 7,887   Registered at the G.P.O. as a Newspaper.   MONDAY, FEBRUARY 25, 1929   One Penny

CHANNEL CRASH

MOBS IN THE BOMBAY RIOTS

The Tamworth in harbour. She was damaged at X.

Damage to the Arundel, in dry dock.

The Southern Railway steamer Arundel was in collision in fog yesterday with a Newcastle collier Tamworth, anchored outside Newhaven Harbour. The Tamworth, sinking, was beached, but at high tide she was towed into harbour. The Arundel made the harbour and her fifty passengers were safely disembarked.

Police chasing Pathans during the rioting, in which 137 people have been killed, in Bombay.

Pathans ready armed for any trouble. Murders, looting and arson were committed by extremists.

The first pictures to reach England of the riots in Bombay. Arising from a strike, the trouble developed into a war between Moslems and Hindus. Military and police had to fire on fourteen occasions to disperse mobs. In addition to the killed, about 800 people were injured.

26

STORM OF PROTEST AGAINST PETROL RAMP

£1,000 PRIZE EVERY WEEK

Daily Mirror

THE DAILY PICTURE PAPER WITH THE LARGEST NET SALE

No. 7,892   Registered at the G.P.O. as a Newspaper.   SATURDAY, MARCH 2, 1929   One Penny

RACING CONTEST COUPON TO-DAY

SKIN PATTERNING

DYNAMITE SHIP BLOWS UP

The steamer Tritonia, of Glasgow, which caught fire and exploded at night in the bay at Buenaventura, Colombia, South America, killing two engineers who stayed on board to try to flood the vessel. Among her cargo were 200 boxes of dynamite. The city of Buenaventura was rocked and damage is reported there.

HARD LUCK!

FAMOUS ATHLETE TO BE MARRIED

A fair visitor to the Riviera waiting for the sun to print a picture on her shoulder. A " transparency " is placed upon the bare skin and the sunrays do the rest.

Ames, the Kent wicket-keeper, who broke a little finger while playing against Victoria. This injury disposes of the question whether he will play in the final Test.

Miss Karen Thamsen, of Copenhagen, engaged to Mr. D. G. A. Lowe.

PILOT SAVED BY PARACHUTE JUMP IN FATAL R.A.F. AIR COLLISION

The wrecked aeroplane from which Sergeant Freeman safely jumped with a parachute after an air collision with a machine piloted by Flying Officer P. N. Sealy-Allin (inset), who was killed. The two machines, which belonged to No. 23 Fighter Squadron, R.A.F., were carrying out formation exercises over Kenley Aerodrome at a height of about 3,000 feet.

Mr. D. G. A. Lowe, the Olympic champion runner, who is to marry Miss Karen Thamsen, a Dane. She has been in England for some years as private secretary to Sir St. Clair Thomson, the surgeon.

EXPLOSIONS AND FIRE AT WOOLWICH ARSENAL

MORE INSURANCE CLAIMS PAID

DailyMirror

THE DAILY PICTURE PAPER WITH THE LARGEST NET SALE

32 PAGES

No. 7,894   Registered at the G.P.O. as a Newspaper.   TUESDAY, MARCH 5, 1929   One Penny

MR. HOOVER BECOMES THE U.S.A. PRESIDENT

Mr. Coolidge retired yesterday from Presidency of United States.

Mr. Herbert Hoover, who became President in his place.

The Capitol at Washington, where President Hoover took the oath yesterday, photographed during the similar ceremony with which President Coolidge began his term of office. Mr. Hoover is an economic expert, who was born forty-five years ago as the son of a village blacksmith in the State of Iowa.

INCOME TAX CLAIM

SAILOR DIES

Admiral of the Fleet Sir Edward Seymour, senior member of the Order of Merit, whose death at the age of eighty-eight was announced yesterday.

Mrs. Bertram Brooke, Dayang Muda of Sarawak, arriving at York House, Kingsway, yesterday, to appear before the Income Tax Commissioners on the contention that she is not a British subject and not liable to pay super-tax.

THE QUEEN VISITS SILVER EXHIBITION

TREATY SENSATION

The Queen leaving Sir Philip Sassoon's house in Park-lane yesterday after viewing a loan exhibition of old English silver plate gathered from many famous collections, in aid of the Royal Northern Hospital.—(" Daily Mirror " photograph.)

Albert Frank Heine, who has been arrested at a Brussels railway station for forgery of the alleged secret Franco-Belgian Treaty published in Holland. He is stated to have confessed.

M. A. NOBLE ON FIFTH TEST MATCH: EXCLUSIVE

ANOTHER PRIZE MYSTERY STORY

DailyMirror

THE DAILY PICTURE PAPER WITH THE LARGEST NET SALE

No. 7,898   Registered at the G.P.O. as a Newspaper.   SATURDAY, MARCH 9, 1929   One Penny

RACING CONTEST COUPON TO-DAY

HOBBS'S 142 IN TEST   "CAPT. BARKER" FREED

Jack Hobbs, who made 142 for England in the first innings in the Test match at Melbourne yesterday, his twelfth century in England v. Australia matches

Mrs. Valerie Smith (in light costume), who for so long masqueraded as "Captain Barker" (as in small picture), leaving Holloway Prison yesterday, when an order for her release was made. She had been detained for contempt of Court in bankruptcy proceedings.—("Daily Mirror.")

Sutcliffe caught by Oldfield for 17 in the fourth Test match at Adelaide

Duckworth cleverly catches Woodfull out for one in the first innings.

These pictures of the thrilling fourth Test match were transmitted from Paris yesterday by the "Daily Mirror's" photo-telegraphy system. It was a match full of surprises and resulted in the closest finish yet produced by the present series, England winning by only twelve runs. This result was largely due to J. C. White's brilliant bowling.

SPRING FASHIONS SPECIAL NUMBER:

EXCLUSIVE PICTURES

NEW £1,000 PICTURE PUZZLE

Daily Mirror

THE DAILY PICTURE PAPER WITH THE LARGEST NET SALE

32 PAGES

No. 7,899   Registered at the G.P.O. as a Newspaper.   MONDAY, MARCH 11, 1929   One Penny

FATAL EXPRESS COLLISION

SPRING STYLES

The scene of the collision outside Darlington Station of an express and a light engine. The guard's van and a luggage van were telescoped, and the guard, Thomas Ringrose, died soon after reaching hospital. Wilfred Carter, driver of the light engine, also died in hospital yesterday. Two men were injured. See also page 16.

DEATH OF VISCOUNT FINLAY

Viscount Finlay, a former Lord Chancellor, who died in London, aged eighty-six, and his son, Mr. Justice Finlay, who succeeds to the title, his daughter-in-law, Lady Finlay, the new Viscountess, and his grand-daughter, Rosalind.

ROBBED BY BANDITS

Miss Doris Clarke, who was seized and gagged by one of three men who entered a Belgravia post office. The other two men robbed the safe and all three escaped in a car. Miss Clarke was found in a state of collapse.

A black satin beauté dress with an inset of the reverse side of the material and white insets on the cuffs. In this spring fashions number the " Daily Mirror " illustrates with exclusive pictures the choicest designs of the coming season. See also pages 16, 17 and 19. Baroque.—(" Daily Mirror.")

30

ANOTHER £1,000 RACING COUPON TO-DAY:

FREE ENTRY

MORE INSURANCE CLAIMS PAID

DailyMirror

THE DAILY PICTURE PAPER WITH THE LARGEST NET SALE

No. 7,900   Registered at the G.P.O. as a Newspaper.   TUESDAY, MARCH 12, 1929   One Penny

32 PAGES

HOTEL FIRE DEATHS

The King Edward Hotel, Hong Kong, where at least thirteen persons, including three Londoners, lost their lives in a great fire yesterday. Two Americans and a Frenchman also perished. The flames swept up the stairs, trapping occupants of upper floors. Mr. and Mrs. James Mitchell, the manager and his wife, are in the centre of the group.

231 MILES AN HOUR!

Major Segrave, who yesterday drove his car Golden Arrow at 231.36 miles per hour.

Major Segrave's wonderful car Golden Arrow, in which the famous driver won back for Britain the world's speed record at Daytona Beach, Florida, with these amazing figures: 231.51 miles per hour for the northward mile and 231.21 miles an hour on the southward run. He took a four miles start, and drove with a brisk wind blowing across the course from the sea. The previous world's record was by Ray Keech, the American with 207.55 miles an hour, driving a Giant Triplex.

M. A. NOBLE ON THE TEST: EXCLUSIVE CABLE

£1,000 PRIZE EVERY WEEK

DailyMirror

THE DAILY PICTURE PAPER WITH THE LARGEST NET SALE

No. 7,901 | Registered at the G.P.O. as a Newspaper. | WEDNESDAY, MARCH 13, 1929 | One Penny

RACING CONTEST COUPON TO-DAY

THE KING IN THE SUNSHINE — FIRST PICTURE

The King, accompanied by the Queen, during a sunshine outing in the grounds of Craigweil House, Bognor. His Majesty spent about an hour in the gardens yesterday but as, in spite of pleasantly warm sun, there was a cool easterly breeze, it was considered advisable that he should remain on the sheltered side of the house. He has benefited much in spirits from his spring weather airings and it is hoped to be able to continue them daily. Another picture of his Majesty in the open air is on page 28.

32

NEW SENSATION AT GARAGE CRIME INQUEST

RACING
CONTEST
COUPON
TO-DAY

DailyMirror

THE DAILY PICTURE PAPER WITH THE LARGEST NET SALE

32 PAGES

No. 7,903 Registered at the G.P.O as a Newspaper. FRIDAY, MARCH 15, 1929 One Penny

LEE BIBLE'S FATAL CRASH—CABLED PICTURE

Captain Malcolm Campbell, who, it is being urged, should abandon his record-breaking plans at Verneuk Pan.

Wreckage of the Triplex car in which Mr. Lee Bible, the American, was killed while trying at Daytona Beach, Florida, to beat Major Segrave's record of 231 m.p.h.—(Telegraphed from Daytona to New York and cabled thence by the "Daily Mirror's" Bartlane process: Western Union transmission.)

Captain Campbell making an examination of Verneuk Pan, which is 400 miles north of Capetown. When it is dry the surface consists of small sections of baked mud.

Mr. Lee Bible in the car just before the start of his fatal trip.—(By Bartlane process; Western Union transmission.)

Mr. J. M. White, the owner of the car in which Mr. Lee Bible crashed.

The Bluebird, Captain Campbell's car, at Capetown on the way to Verneuk Pan.

Numerous "Daily Mirror" readers have put forward the contention that, in order to avoid the risk of a repetition of the disaster to Mr. Lee Bible, Captain Malcolm Campbell's proposed attempt to create a new speed record for Britain should be abandoned. The track he has chosen at Verneuk Pan, South Africa, has, they state, treacherous mirages and a dangerous surface for high-speed driving. Mr. Kaye Don, the racing motorist, is among those who urge the danger of the enterprise.

FOCH'S SECRET WAR HISTORY

BY MAJOR-GEN. SIR F. MAURICE ON PAGE 13

LOMBARD
THE BEST
CITY GUIDE

DailyMirror

THE DAILY PICTURE PAPER WITH THE LARGEST NET SALE

No. 7,908 | Registered at the G.P.O. as a Newspaper. | THURSDAY, MARCH 21, 1929 | One Penny

32 PAGES

DEATH OF FOCH, THE VICTORY MAKER

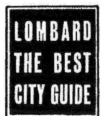

Marshal Foch in the great Victory march through London in July, 1919.

Just before the signing of the Armistice in 1918.

Revisiting the trenches in 1924.

Marshal Foch, who led the Allies to victory, has died in Paris.

The " Daily Mirror " regrets to announce that Marshal of France Ferdinand Foch, the brilliant general who commanded the whole of the Allied Armies on the Western Front during the later stages of the Great War, died yesterday at his home in the Rue de Grenelle, Paris. He had been dangerously ill for some time. Marshal Foch was born at Tarbes in 1851, and before the outbreak of the war he had become a divisional commander. During the war his advance was rapid, and in 1918 he became the Allied Generalissimo and Marshal of France. By his subtle strategy and forceful methods of attack he finally broke the German front and put the enemy to disordered flight.

34

£1,000 RACING FORECAST COUPON ON PAGE 31

NEW
£1,000
PICTURE
PUZZLE

DailyMirror

THE DAILY PICTURE PAPER WITH THE LARGEST NET SALE

No. 7,911 — Registered at the G.P.O. as a Newspaper. — MONDAY, MARCH 25, 1929 — One Penny

32 PAGES

MARSHAL FOCH UNDER THE ARC DE TRIOMPHE

The widow and daughters of Marshal Foch about to pass the coffin as it lies in state beneath the Arc de Triomphe. In the foreground is the Unknown Soldier's tomb.

Marshal Foch's coffin being taken from the house in which he died.

A guard of honour saluting as the body arrives at the arch.

Placed on a gun-carriage and draped with a Tricolor flag, the coffin containing Marshal Foch's body was placed under the Arc de Triomphe yesterday. He is the first Frenchman to be so honoured since Victor Hugo, if the Unknown Soldier be regarded as a symbol rather than an individual. At night four torches bathed the lying-in-state with a soft glow. Reverent crowds filed past from the highest to the humblest in the land. The funeral will take place to-morrow. See also pages 16 and 17.

BRILLIANT NEW SERIAL BEGINS ON WEDNESDAY

BEST FREE FAMILY INSURANCE

DailyMirror

THE DAILY PICTURE PAPER WITH THE LARGEST NET SALE

RACING CONTEST COUPON TO-DAY

No. 7,915   Registered at the G.P.O. as a Newspaper.   SATURDAY, MARCH 30, 1929   One Penny

GREAT START FOR YEAR'S FIRST HOLIDAY

Joyfully hoisting the mainsail at the outset of a cruise on the Norfolk Broad...

Deck chairs in mass formation on the pier at Southend.

A dense crowd on the promenade at Brighton yesterday.

The fine weather for Easter, forecast by the experts, having materialised, there has been a rush from London and other towns to seaside, country and the Continent which reached record proportions. Railways, air lines and steamers worked at highest pressure, and roads were packed with all manner of vehicles. A continuation of warm sunshine is promised, and with the nearest rain a thousand miles away, "set fair" is to remain Britain's happy motto till after the holiday. (See also pages 12 and 13.)

NEW MYSTERY SERIAL STARTS ON WEDNESDAY

NEW £1,000 PICTURE PUZZLE

DailyMirror

THE DAILY PICTURE ● PAPER WITH THE LARGEST NET SALE

No. 7,916   Registered at the G.P.O. as a Newspaper.   MONDAY, APRIL 1, 1929   One Penny

RACING CONTEST COUPON TO-DAY

FRENCH EX-SERVICE PILGRIMS IN LONDON

General Gouraud saluting the Cenotaph at the head of the French Legion pilgrims He placed a wreath there on behalf of the ex-Servicemen of France.

Banners of the French and British Legions dipped in salute during the ceremony in Whitehall. The French ex-Servicemen are grouped nearer the camera.

Nine hundred French ex-Servicemen, headed by General Gouraud, the famous one-armed war leader, paid tribute in London yesterday to their fallen British comrades. Their coming is by way of a return visit after last year's great British Legion pilgrimage to the battlefields. The delegates attended an official reception in Westminster Hall, rendered homage at the tomb of the Unknown Warrior, and marched to the Cenotaph.—("Daily Mirror" photographs.) See also page 24.

THREE BROTHERS POISONED BY ACCIDENT

£1,000 PRIZE EVERY WEEK

Daily Mirror

THE DAILY PICTURE PAPER WITH THE LARGEST NET SALE

No. 7,923   Registered at the G.P.O. as a Newspaper.   TUESDAY, APRIL 9, 1929   One Penny

MORE INSURANCE CLAIMS PAID

BOMB DRAMA IN INDIAN PARLIAMENT HOUSE

Sir John Simon, who was present but unhurt.

Sir George Schuster, Finance Member, one of the injured.

CHILDREN IN FATAL LORRY SMASH

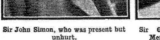

The van of the meat lorry after the accident.

The scene of the bomb outrage. Inset left—Mr. Patel. Inset right—Mr. Raghvendra Rao.

Henry Burns, aged three, who received head injuries, with his mother.

Henry Martin, aged seven, who was killed.

When the driver of a meat lorry swerved in Robin Hood-lane, Poplar, the van left the chassis and crashed to the pavement. Henry Martin was pinned underneath and killed, and his brother Thomas, and Henry Burns were hurt.—("Daily Mirror" photographs.)

An aerial view of the Parliament House at New Delhi, where two bombs were hurled during a sitting of the Indian Legislative Assembly Benches were blown to pieces and among the injured are Sir George Schuster and Mr. Raghvendra Rao. Mr. Patel, the President, had just got up to give his ruling on a controversial measure when the explosions occurred.

LORD ROTHERMERE'S ELECTION WARNING

SEE
PAGE 3

**BEST
FREE
FAMILY
INSURANCE**

DailyMirror

THE DAILY PICTURE PAPER WITH THE LARGEST NET SALE

No. 7,925   Registered at the G.P.O. as a Newspaper.   THURSDAY, APRIL 11, 1929   One Penny

**£1,000
PRIZE
EVERY
WEEK**

£100,000 LEGACY FOR EX-NAVAL OFFICER

Commander Claude Philip de Crespigny (left), a retired naval officer, who receives a legacy of £100,000 under the will of Princess Hatzfeldt, who was one of the richest women in the world.

Princess Hatzfeldt, who was an American by birth, and was left £15,000,000 by her uncle, a railway magnate. She died in London in December, having been a famous beauty and hostess in the reigns of King Edward and Queen Victoria. She also had a residence in France.

JUST MISSED GETTING OVER—GIRL RIDER'S MISHAP

Pippin just fails to carry Miss Cecily Nickall over the brook during the Grafton Hunt's hunter trials held yesterday at Greens Norton, near Towcester, Northamptonshire.

SHOT WITH FRIEND'S REVOLVER

Mrs. Honoria Gordon, niece of Lord Ruthven, at the inquest on whom, at Paddington yesterday, a verdict of Suicide while of unsound mind was returned. She shot herself with a woman friend's revolver in the same friend's flat.

39

WHAT IS MR. CHURCHILL'S BUDGET SECRET?

RACING CONTEST COUPON TO-DAY

DailyMirror
THE DAILY PICTURE PAPER WITH THE LARGEST NET SALE

No. 7,928   Registered at the G.P.O. as a Newspaper.   MONDAY, APRIL 15, 1929   One Penny

NEW £1,000 PICTURE PUZZLE

FOUNDLING HOSPITAL SAVED

PEER'S DEATH

For one month in the year British boy scouts are to have the use of the site as a camping ground.

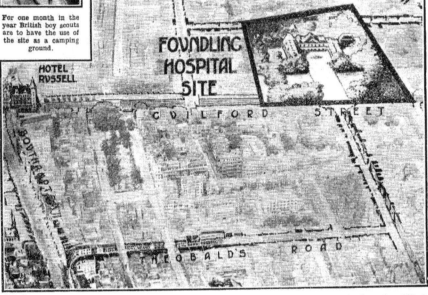

Lord Mostyn, who has died at Hove, aged seventy-three, after an operation. Right—his elder son, Mr. E. Lloyd-Mostyn, the new peer.

GRANTED FREE PARDON

The site of the Foundling Hospital in Bloomsbury, which has been saved, for the present at least, by the action of Lord Rothermere. A contract is being prepared between him and the owners which provides for the sale of the site, to be used as a children's park, for £525,000. Lord Rothermere is paying a deposit of £50,000, and 5½ per cent. per annum interest on the remainder until June 30, 1931. If by that time the purchase is not completed the site will revert to the vendors. Lord Rothermere will give a further £50,000 towards the purchase money, making £100,000 in addition to the interest.

Miss Alice Silverthorne, of Chicago, who, sentenced to six months' imprisonment in 1927 on a charge of shooting Mr. Raymond de Trafford, has, it is reported from Paris, been granted a free pardon. See news story.

ARRIVAL OF FIRST INDIA-ENGLAND AIR MAIL—TO KARACHI AND BACK IN 14½ DAYS

Passengers from Karachi on the first India to London air mail on their arrival, two minutes ahead of scheduled time, at Croydon yesterday: Sir Geoffrey Salmond (dark suit), Hon. Eve Chetwynd, Sir Vyell Vyvyan and Viscount Chetwynd. Right, Unloading mailbags from India. Air Marshal Sir V. Vyvyan left London on the inaugural London to India flight on March 30, and has made the double journey in fourteen and a half days, faster than the journey had been done in one direction hitherto.

40

DUTIES ON TEA AND BETTING ABOLISHED

£1,000 PRIZE EVERY WEEK

DailyMirror

THE DAILY PICTURE PAPER WITH THE LARGEST NET SALE

No. 7,929 | Registered at the G.P.O. as a Newspaper. | TUESDAY, APRIL 16, 1929 | One Penny

MORE INSURANCE CLAIMS PAID

MR. CHURCHILL'S BUDGET ESCORT

Mr. Winston Churchill carrying his Budget in the famous Chancellor's dispatch-case, and, with his wife and daughter beside him, escorted by a policeman and a big crowd from Downing-street to the House of Commons yesterday for his Budget statement. He announced that the tea duty would be abolished so that there would be a reduction of 4d. per lb. in price to the consumer. The betting tax, he said, was more trouble than it was worth and would cease, its place being taken by a £10 licence for bookmakers, with a charge of £40 on every bookmaker's telephone. A tax on totalisators would produce £900,000 per year.

41

£1,000 AGAIN OFFERED FOR A DERBY FORECAST

£1,000 PRIZE EVERY WEEK

DailyMirror

THE DAILY PICTURE PAPER WITH THE LARGEST NET SALE

No. 7,931 | Registered at the G.P.O. as a Newspaper. | THURSDAY, APRIL 18, 1929 | One Penny

BIGGEST AND BEST PICTURE PAPER

MASTER OF SEMPILL'S FLIGHT TO LUNCHEON

The Master of Sempill and his passenger, the Dowager Lady Swaythling, after the flight.

The seaplane in which Colonel the Master of Sempill, heir of Lord Sempill, flew yesterday from Hendon, N.W., to attend a luncheon at a West End hotel taxi-ing towards Waterloo Bridge after alighting on the Thames.

VACCINATION SUSPENDED

Putting up a notice at Victoria Station.

A visitor to France being vaccinated on landing.

The order made by the French Government that all travellers from England must be vaccinated before landing in France has been suspended until further notice—but not before it had occasioned a great deal of confusion. Many intending visitors had themselves vaccinated yesterday.

NAVAL GUARD OF HONOUR AT WEDDING OF EARL'S NIECE

Lieutenant Clive Loehnis, R.N., son of the late Mr. H. W. Loehnis, and his bride, Miss Rosemary Ryder, niece of the Earl of Harrowby, after their wedding at St. Margaret's, Westminster, yesterday.

£1,000 DERBY CONTEST: FIRST COUPON TO-DAY

CLOCKS FORWARD AN HOUR TO-NIGHT

DailyMirror

THE DAILY PICTURE PAPER WITH THE LARGEST NET SALE

No. 7,933   Registered at the G.P.O. as a Newspaper.   SATURDAY, APRIL 20, 1929   One Penny

LOMBARD THE BEST CITY GUIDE

PEER'S TRAGEDY   CAMPBELL TO TRY TO-DAY

Lord Revelstoke, chairman of the sub-committee of experts who have been discussing reparations with the Germans, died from a sudden heart attack yesterday in his flat at Paris. He had had an exceptionally anxious time the day before owing to the deadlock with Germany over war debts.

Captain Malcolm Campbell, who will to-day attempt at Verneuk Pan, South Africa, to beat the motor-car speed record of 231 m.p.h. made by Major Segrave, with his wife and children.

The 1,000 horse-power car, Bluebird, in which Captain Malcolm Campbell will to-day make his attempt. He yesterday reached an unofficial speed of 210 m.p.h. in a one-way trial and touched 215 m.p.h. During the run the car struck a bump and travelled 30ft. without touching the track, which is a dried-up lake 3,000ft. above sea level. The prepared surface extends for fifteen miles and has been described as being "as smooth as a billiards table."

43

£1,000 DERBY CONTEST: COUPON TO-DAY ON PAGE 27

BEST FREE FAMILY INSURANCE

DailyMirror

THE DAILY PICTURE ● PAPER WITH THE LARGEST NET SALE

No. 7,936 | Registered at the G.P.O. as a Newspaper. | WEDNESDAY, APRIL 24, 1929 | One Penny

LOMBARD THE BEST CITY GUIDE

GRETNA GREEN RUNAWAYS AT WINDERMERE

The runaway couple in the grounds of a hotel at Windermere.

ZEEBRUGGE RAID ANNIVERSARY

Admiral Sir Roger Keyes, who was in command of the operations against Zeebrugge and Ostend on April 23, 1918, placing a wreath at the Cenotaph yesterday on the anniversary of the immortal raid.

Mr. Hector Mappin and his nineteen-year-old heiress bride, Miss Olive Ridsdel, on the shores of Lake Windermere, standing by the motor-car in which they made their romantic flight from Essex to the North. They were married at Gretna Green smithy.

WOMAN "FINANCIAL WIZARD" AT BLACKMAIL TRIAL

Mme. Hanau, the woman financier who is awaiting trial for the alleged "Gazette du Franc" frauds, at the Paris law courts where she was a witness in a case concerning a series of charges in which a French journalist is accused of having blackmailed her.

44

£105,000 THANK-OFFERING FOR KING'S RECOVERY

CUP FINAL PAGES OF PICTURES

DailyMirror
THE DAILY PICTURE PAPER WITH THE LARGEST NET SALE

No. 7,940   Registered at the G.P.O. as a Newspaper.   MONDAY, APRIL 29, 1929   One Penny

£1,000 DERBY COUPON TO-DAY

FIVE KILLED IN BLAZING MOTOR-COACH

Ruins of the motor-coach which caught fire on the Reading road, near Twyford, Berkshire, late on Saturday night. Four people were burned to death on the spot and a fifth died in hospital yesterday. Inset, Mrs. Bidmead, who is believed to be among the dead.

The coach overturned and several occupants were trapped inside it. Some passengers escaped by smashing windows. The party had been to see the Reading-Chelsea football match at Stamford Bridge. See pages 14 and 15.

Mrs. William Herbert, of Smalls Cottages, London-street, Reading, who was killed, and her husband, who was severely injured and is in hospital.

Mrs. Emma Moore, of Coney-place, Reading, who died in hospital yesterday, and Mr. J. C. Moore, of Toley-place, Reading, who was injured.

THE CUP GOES NORTH AGAIN

The Prince of Wales presenting to Seddon, the Bolton captain, the F.A. Cup which Bolton Wanderers won at Wembley by beating Portsmouth by two goals to nil. See also page 28.

GIFT OF £105,000

The Earl of Donoughmore, who will be treasurer of a fund for hospitals, as a thankoffering for the King's recovery from his recent severe illness, which an anonymous donor has opened with a gift of £105,000.

MORE INSURANCE CLAIMS PAID: REGISTER NOW

£100 CROSSWORD PUZZLE

DailyMirror

THE DAILY PICTURE PAPER WITH THE LARGEST NET SALE

BIGGEST AND BEST PICTURE PAPER

No. 7,941   Registered at the G.P.O. as a Newspaper.   TUESDAY, APRIL 30, 1929   One Penny

FAMOUS WRECKS OF 1,900 YEARS AGO

SISTERS' ROMANCE

Miss Adele Biddulph, elder daughter of Lord and Lady Biddulph, who is engaged to Mr. Henry Yorke. The engagement of her sister Mary was announced last week.

DUKE'S UNCLE

Lord Arthur Grosvenor, uncle of the Duke of Westminster and the heir presumptive to the title, who has died at Broxton, Chester.

The first picture of one of Caligula's two galleys, revealed by pumping 1,900 years after they were sunk in Lake Nemi, the crater of an extinct volcano near Rome.

Remains of the other galley. Legend declares that Caligula, the mad Emperor of Rome, deliberately sank the two galleys, which were pleasure palaces, with his guests on board in order to crown an orgy. They are believed to contain precious metals.—("Daily Mirror" exclusive photographs.)

HONOUR FOR GENERAL BOOTH

General Bramwell Booth, the former chief of the Salvation Army, who, it was announced yesterday, has been made by the King a member of the Order of Companions of Honour. With him is his wife.—("Daily Mirror" photograph.)

46

THE DAILY MIRROR, Wednesday, May 1, 1929

£1,000 DERBY CONTEST—COUPON TO-DAY

LOMBARD THE BEST CITY GUIDE

Daily Mirror

THE DAILY PICTURE PAPER WITH THE LARGEST NET SALE

No. 7,942   Registered at the G.P.O. as a Newspaper.   WEDNESDAY, MAY 1, 1929   One Penny

£1,000 PICTURE PUZZLE WEEKLY

PRINCE FOUNDS £200,000 DENTAL CLINIC

The Prince of Wales speaking yesterday at a ceremony during which he laid the foundation-stone of a model dental clinic in Gray's Inn-road. Mr Stanley Baldwin is also on the platform. The clinic is the gift of Mr. George Eastman, the wealthy American, and it is estimated that it will cost £200,000.

COUNTESS DIES IN COTTAGE AFTER A CAR COLLISION

BOY'S TWO PICTURES AT R.A.

The car in which the Countess of Powis (inset) was being driven from Powis Castle to London, when it became involved in a collision with another car at Towcester, Northamptonshire. Lady Powis, carried fainting to a nearby cottage, died shortly afterwards, apparently from shock.

Sylvain Kluska, a seventeen-year-old art student, who had two pictures accepted for this year's Academy, working in his home in Little Turner-street, Commercial-road.—(" Daily Mirror " photograph.)

MAY DAY SHOOTING AND RIOTING IN BERLIN

LAUGH WITH THE PATER DAILY

DailyMirror

THE DAILY PICTURE PAPER WITH THE LARGEST NET SALE

BEST FREE FAMILY INSURANCE

No. 7,943   Registered at the G.P.O. as a Newspaper.   THURSDAY, MAY 2, 1929   One Penny

VANISHED SENTRY MYSTERY

Changing guard in front of one of the sentry-boxes outside Buckingham Palace. From one of these Guardsman Sivwright, a private in the 1st Battalion Scots Guards, vanished while on sentry duty. Scotland Yard have been asked to co-operate in the search for him.

£3,000 REFUSED

The Rev. Joseph Shepherd, of Islington Chapel, who states that no woman in his district will accept £3,000 a year to spend on herself and a luxurious home in America. This offer was made by a wealthy American business man who wanted to find an English wife

"HAPHAZARD" STATEMENT

Mr. Thomas Sidney, who at the resumed inquest on his sister, Miss Vera Sidney, exhumed at Croydon, said yesterday that a statement to the police was made by him "in a haphazard way." He added he did not then know that her death was being inquired into. He was closely questioned by the coroner.

ROYAL SCOTS OFFICER WEDS

Mr. Stanford Bunn, Royal Scots, son of the late Mr. H. H. Bunn, and his bride, Miss Ursula Russell, daughter of Lieutenant-Colonel the Hon. Bertrand Russell, after their wedding yesterday at St. Mary's, Cadogan-street.

3,000 MAY DAY ARRESTS

Gendarmes searching passers-by in Paris yesterday. Three thousand preventive arrests were made to avoid May Day demonstrations by Communists and the city remained quiet.—(By "Daily Mirror" photo-telephony.)

THE DAILY MIRROR. Monday, May 6, 1929

GREAT NEW EVENING PAPER FOR THE NORTH

SUMMER FASHIONS NUMBER

DailyMirror

THE DAILY PICTURE PAPER WITH THE LARGEST NET SALE

No. 7,946   Registered at the G.P.O. as a Newspaper   MONDAY, MAY 6, 1929   One Penny

32 PAGES

GREAT NON-STOP FLIGHT

SUMMER FASHIONS

Squadron-Leader A. G. Jones-Williams, R.A.F., at Karachi just after landing from the giant Fairey monoplane in which with Flight-Lieutenant N. H. Jenkins he accomplished the first non-stop flight to India. His first words to those who welcomed him were, "We have landed her to have another smack."

A BUS THAT VERY NEARLY DIVED

ATTACKED

Mrs. Rose James, of Slinfold, Sussex, who was attacked and seriously injured while travelling in a train between Horsham and Guildford. A man was detained.

IN LONDON

Miss Helen Wills, the lawn tennis champion, photographed at Victoria last night on her arrival in England for her forthcoming presentation at Court.

A bus which, after collision with another vehicle, crashed through railings on the Wey bridge at Weybridge, so that its front overhung the river. One woman passenger had a cut leg.

A charming summer ensemble of navy blue and orange patterned chiffon with a yoke of fine ecru guipure lace and a jabot of net to match. Other pictures of fashions for the summer are on pages 16 and 17. Baroque.— ("Daily Mirror" photograph.)

MORE INSURANCE CLAIMS PAID: REGISTER NOW

BLOOD ROYAL TO-DAY

Daily Mirror

THE DAILY PICTURE PAPER WITH THE LARGEST NET SALE

No. 7,953 Registered at the G.P.O. as a Newspaper. TUESDAY, MAY 14, 1929 One Penny

32 PAGES

PARTY LEADERS BUSY WITH THE ELECTION

Mr. Lloyd George speaking regarding the Government's White Paper at the National Liberal Club.

Mr. Baldwin, preceded by Mrs. Baldwin, on his arrival at Truro. He declared he started his campaign confident of victory.

Mr. Winston Churchill in a characteristic attitude during his first meeting at Epping yesterday.

Mr. Lloyd George in his striking speech yesterday, accused the Government of taking an "unprecedented and unwarranted step in issuing a document with the seal of the Crown as a political pamphlet." He was speaking to Liberal candidates and agents. Mr. Stanley Baldwin at Truro opened his tour in the West.

NURSES CHAIR TWO FAMOUS GIRL PLAYERS AT THE OPENING OF LAWN TENNIS COURT

Miss Betty Nuthall (left) and Miss Joan Ridley, who played exhibition lawn tennis sets, in the arms of nurses of the Lambeth Board of Guardians' Institution at Brook-street, Kennington, yesterday, when Miss Nuthall opened a new lawn tennis court for the use of the staff. Their visit excited the greatest interest.

BEGIN OUR GREAT SERIAL, 'BLOOD ROYAL,' TO-DAY

£1,000
DERBY
COUPON
TO-DAY

DailyMirror

THE DAILY PICTURE ● PAPER WITH THE LARGEST NET SALE

No. 7,954 | Registered at the G.P.O. as a Newspaper. | WEDNESDAY, MAY 15, 1929 | One Penny

32 PAGES

PRINCE OF WALES'S VISIT TO THE NORTH

The Prince of Wales presenting a standard to the Durham branch of the British Legion yesterday.

The Prince talking to Mr. Conner Graham, aged ninety-six, at Durham.

Inspecting his guard of honour at North-East Coast Exhibition.

The Prince of Wales visited Durham yesterday mainly to see the work for the preservation of Durham Castle, which is threatened by the undermining of the foundation of the Western wall. He also paid a visit to the British Legion there, and Mr. Conner Graham, a veteran aged ninety-six, was among his guard of honour. The Prince went on to Newcastle and there opened the great North-East Coast Exhibition, which he described as the "challenge of the North-East to the world."

DO NOT MISS "BLOOD ROYAL" ON PAGE 17

£1,000 DERBY COUPON DAILY

DailyMirror

THE DAILY PICTURE PAPER WITH THE LARGEST NET SALE

No. 7,955 — Registered at the G.P.O. as a Newspaper. — THURSDAY, MAY 16, 1929 — One Penny

LOMBARD THE BEST CITY GUIDE

THE KING'S WELCOME AT WINDSOR

The King's car about to enter Castle Rise, Windsor, after his Majesty had been welcomed on arrival from Bognor yesterday by the Mayor, Lieut.-Colonel Stephen Wright (x). In his car the King was accompanied by the Queen, and they were loudly cheered at every town and village en route. At Windsor they found so many people from so many places to welcome his Majesty after his recovery of health that the great cheers he received in the streets of the royal borough may be said to represent a national welcome. Windsor has not been so crowded since their Majesties' return there after their coronation. See also pages 14 and 15.—(" Daily Mirror " photographs.)

THE DAILY MIRROR, Thursday, May 23, 1929.

POLICE SENSATION: MORE OFFICERS SUSPENDED

LAUGH
DAILY
WITH THE
PATER

Daily Mirror

THE DAILY PICTURE ● PAPER WITH THE LARGEST NET SALE

No. 7,961   Registered at the G.P.O. as a Newspaper.   THURSDAY, MAY 23, 1929   One Penny

LOMBARD
THE BEST
CITY GUIDE

THE PRINCE OPENS NOTTINGHAM'S CIVIC H.Q.

The crowded scene outside the Council House, Nottingham's new civic headquarters, when the Prince of Wales arrived to declare the building open yesterday.

Talking to Mr. Caffrey, V.C. (x), in the guard of honour.

The Prince of Wales declaring the Council House open. Beside him stands the Lord Mayor.

The Prince of Wales flew from Hendon to Nottingham yesterday to attend the Notts Agricultural Show and to open with a golden key the Council House, erected at a cost of £250,000. Commenting on Nottingham's preservation of its charm, he remarked that " a good appearance is good business." At the show the Prince's exhibits of shorthorns from his Notts farm won nine prizes. In the evening he flew back to Hendon aerodrome.— (" Daily Mirror " photographs.)

53

DOCTOR'S WIFE GIVES HER LIFE TO SAVE CHILD

MOTOR ARTICLE TO-DAY

DailyMirror

THE DAILY PICTURE PAPER WITH THE LARGEST NET SALE

No. 7,962   Registered at the G.P.O. as a Newspaper.   FRIDAY, MAY 24, 1929   One Penny

BEST FREE FAMILY INSURANCE

LONDON'S HEAT WAVE: 81 DEGS. IN THE SHADE

A welcome refresher in the Thames near Lambeth Bridge during London's heat wave yesterday.

A healthgiving sunbath for smiling children on the roof of the Aldwych Crèche. The morning temperature was 73.

Miss Meyers playing without stockings in the doubles of the Surrey lawn tennis championships at Surbiton.

On the brink of a bathing pool on a roof rock garden in London.

The temperature of 81 degrees in the shade in Central London yesterday was only 5 degrees below the highest reading for May, recorded in the heat wave of 1922. Last night's forecast predicted rather high to moderate temperature with bright periods and local thunderstorms. The week-end forecast is " warm, rather unsettled, local thunderstorms."

THE DAILY MIRROR, Saturday, May 25, 1929.

POLICE CENTENARY: TO-DAY'S GREAT MARCH

£1,000 DERBY COUPON DAILY

DailyMirror

THE DAILY PICTURE PAPER WITH THE LARGEST NET SALE

No. 7,963 | Registered at the G.P.O. as a Newspaper. | SATURDAY, MAY 25, 1929 | One Penny

BEST FREE FAMILY INSURANCE

TO-DAY'S GREAT LONDON POLICE CENTENARY

Old Scotland Yard as it appeared several generations ago, before the police occupied it.

The department at New Scotland Yard where criminal records are stored.

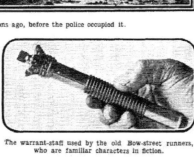

The warrant-staff used by the old Bow-street runners, who are familiar characters in fiction.

Searching for lost umbrellas at the new lost property office in Lambeth.

Debris from a wall blown into the street by an explosion which occurred at Scotland Yard during the Fenian activities.

Before the introduction of the familiar blue helmet—police on parade at Lewisham in 1845.

To-day in celebration of the centenary of the Metropolitan Police, the Prince of Wales will march at the head of a force of 12,000 police in Hyde Park. The Metropolitan Police were founded in 1829 by Sir Robert Peel to consolidate under one control services hitherto rendered by night watchmen, parish constables, the Bow-street runners and military troops. At that time there was one criminal to every twenty-two of the population. Another picture is on pages 12 and 13.

55

THE DAILY MIRROR, Friday, May 31, 1929.

FIRST RESULTS OF BATTLE OF THE VOTES

LOMBARD
THE BEST
CITY GUIDE

DailyMirror

THE DAILY PICTURE ⏺ PAPER WITH THE LARGEST NET SALE

No. 7,968   Registered at the G.P.O. as a Newspaper.   FRIDAY, MAY 31, 1929   One Penny

MOTOR
ARTICLE
TO-DAY

SPLIT VOTE HELPS THE SOCIALISTS

Mr. H. G. Williams, Parliamentary-Secretary, Board of Trade, defeated at Reading by a Socialist.

Sir P. Sassoon, Under-Secretary Air Ministry, defeated two women at Hythe.

Mr. Ben Tillett won North Salford for Socialists on a split vote.

Sir Robert Newman (Ind. Con.), who was re-elected at Exeter

Sir W. Joynson-Hicks had a majority of 5,966 at Twickenham against two other candidates.

Mr. J. Toole won Salford South for the Socialists.

Captain R. C. Bourne retained Oxford City for Conservatives.

Captain E. Wallace, re-elected Conservative member for Hornsey.

Mr. A. Harbord scored Liberal gain at Great Yarmouth.

The Hon. Mary Pickford (Conservative), defeated at Farnworth.

It soon became evident last night that the division of the Anti-Socialist forces was giving seats to the Socialists. The first to fall in this manner was North Salford, where Mr. Ben Tillett, although he polled only 17,333 votes against a combined Conservative and Liberal vote of 20,214, was elected in a constituency which in the last Parliament was Conservative. Mr. Arthur Henderson, who was Home Secretary in the Socialist Government, retained Burnley with 23,091 votes, although 32,639 ballot papers were adverse to him. Similar tales came from Ashton-under-Lyne, Wakefield, Dewsbury, West Salford and other industrial areas. Other election pictures on pages 12, 13 and 24.

THE DAILY MIRROR, Wednesday, June 5, 1929.

MR. MACDONALD TO SEE THE KING TO-DAY

HORSES FOR TO-DAY'S "MOST OPEN" DERBY

Mr. S. B. Joel's Kopi leaving the train in which it had travelled to Epsom.

Mrs. Corlette Glorney, an American, the only woman owner with a horse in the great race. Her candidate is Posterity.

Mr. Jinks, 2,000 Guineas winner, and its jockey, H. Beasley

Lord Derby, the owner of Hunter's Moon, won the race in 1924.

Lord Astor, who will have Cragadour and Cavendo carrying his colours.

Hunter's Moon and T. Weston, its Derby jockey.

Not within living memory has the Derby been so open as the race for the Turf's blue riband which will be run to-day at Epsom. This is owing to several of the most fancied candidates having been under clouds at some time of their training. Mr. Jinks was favourite yesterday afternoon, but in the evening Cragadour again took first place in the betting at 7 to 1. Hunter's Moon, Kopi and Gay Day all have a large following of admirers. Other Derby pictures on pages 14 and 15.

57

THE DAILY MIRROR, Thursday, June 6, 1929

WOMEN'S LUCK IN THE DERBY SWEEPSTAKES

NEW £500 RACING CONTEST

DailyMirror

THE DAILY PICTURE PAPER WITH THE LARGEST NET SALE

No. 7,973   Registered at the G.P.O. as a Newspaper.   THURSDAY, JUNE 6, 1929   One Penny

32 PAGES

TRIGO'S THRILLING DERBY VICTORY

Above, the exciting finish of the Derby, won by a length and a half by Mr. W. Barnett's Trigo, a 33-1 chance, from Lord Woolavington's Walter Gay (100-8). Brienz (50-1) was third J. Marshall rode the winner. Below, Kopi, Mr. S. B. Joel's horse, falling on going down the hill to Tattenham Corner. Its jockey, F. Winter, seen near the rails, was unhurt. The horse came in after the race riderless. Hunter's Moon led until half-way down the hill, but neither Mr. Jinks, the favourite, nor Gay Day ever occupied a prominent position. Cragadour's jockey made a desperate effort in the straight. See also pages 14. 16, 17, 26 and 32.—(" Daily Mirror " photographs.)

58

BEST FREE FAMILY INSURANCE: REGISTER NOW

£500
RACING
COUPON
TO-DAY

DailyMirror

THE DAILY PICTURE PAPER WITH THE LARGEST NET SALE

No. 7,974 — Registered at the G.P.O. as a Newspaper. — FRIDAY, JUNE 7, 1929 — One Penny

32 PAGES

SIR W. DAVISON MARRIED

Miss Constance Marriot, the bride.

Sir William Davison, M.P., who won a strange election fight at South Kensington by a majority of over 20,000, was married yesterday to Miss Constance Marriot at St. Ethelburga's, Bishopsgate.

NEW ERUPTION OF VESUVIUS

Masses of incandescent matter and clouds of steam thrown up by Vesuvius during its present disastrous eruption. These are the first pictures to reach London.

BABY PRINCESS AT ROYAL TOURNAMENT

The Duke and Duchess of York, followed by Princess Elizabeth, in the arms of her nurse, arriving at the Royal Tournament at Olympia yesterday, when the Princess was enthralled by the colourful spectacle. See also page 16.

The great lava stream pouring from Vesuvius. The eruption has already destroyed the village of Barre and seriously threatens two others. A wide area has been evacuated by the terrified inhabitants.—("Daily Mirror" photographs.)

EX-CABINET MINISTER'S POST IN THE CITY

READER WINS £1,000 PRIZE

DailyMirror
THE DAILY PICTURE PAPER WITH THE LARGEST NET SALE

No. 7,975   Registered at the G.P.O. as a Newspaper.   SATURDAY, JUNE 8, 1929   One Penny

RACING CONTEST COUPON DAILY

WOMAN IN THE CABINET FOR FIRST TIME

Mr. MacDonald, who has announced his Cabinet

Mr. Arthur Henderson becomes Foreign Secretary.

Mr. J. H. Thomas is to be Lord Privy Seal.

Mr. Philip Snowden, Chancellor of the Exchequer

Mr. Sidney Webb, Dominions Secretary, with peerage

Miss Margaret Bondfield, as Minister of Labour, becomes the first woman Cabinet Minister in a British Government.

Mr. H. B. Lees-Smith, to be Postmaster-General.

Captain Wedgwood Benn, the Secretary for India.

Sir Oswald Mosley, Chancellor of Duchy of Lancaster.

Mr. W. A. Jowitt, K.C., to be the Attorney-General.

Mr. J. B. Melville, K.C., becomes Solicitor-General.

Miss Margaret Bondfield has the honour of becoming Britain's first woman Cabinet Minister, for in Mr. Ramsay MacDonald's second Socialist Government, the personnel of which was announced last night, she becomes Minister of Labour. Mr. W. Jowitt, K.C., who was elected as a Liberal at Preston, but has now joined the Socialist Party, becomes Attorney-General, and Mr. Sidney Webb will return to Parliament as Secretary for the Dominions with a seat in the House of Lords. Captain Wedgwood Benn becomes Secretary for India and Sir Oswald Mosley is Chancellor of the Duchy of Lancaster. Other political pictures will be found on page 24.

60

OUTBOARD MOTOR-BOAT RACING CONTEST: PAGE 3

NEW £1,000 PICTURE PUZZLE

Daily Mirror

THE DAILY PICTURE PAPER WITH THE LARGEST NET SALE

No. 7,976 — Registered at the G.P.O. as a Newspaper. — MONDAY, JUNE 10, 1929 — One Penny

BEST FREE FAMILY INSURANCE

OCEAN FLIGHT HOPS

RAIL COACH CUT IN TWO BY TRAIN

Lieutenant Floden and M. Ljunclund (taller), who, with Captain Ahrenberg (inset), are on a flight, started yesterday, from Stockholm to New York in stages, via Iceland, Greenland and Canada.

A Sentinel steam coach cut in two in collision with an excursion train yesterday near Doncaster. The front portion, in which were the driver and fireman, has crashed down the embankment beside the line. The rest of the coach is tilted at a dangerous angle. Five people were injured.

BUS TOP DESTROYED BY BRIDGE—NINE PEOPLE INJURED

The L.G.O.C. covered omnibus, the top of which was destroyed when it struck a Southern Railway bridge over Penge-lane, S.E., yesterday. Nine people were injured. The bus was running on a new route from Acton to West Wickham, Kent, and turned into Penge-lane instead of Green-lane. Seven of the injured were taken to hospital.

INDIA AND BACK BY AIR

Mrs. A. Cleaver on return to Croydon yesterday from a flight to Karachi and back, and Captain Drew, the pilot on the last lap. Mrs. Cleaver is daughter of Mr. H. M. Pollock, the Minister of Finance of Northern Ireland.

61

THE DAILY MIRROR, Tuesday, June 11, 1929.

MORE INSURANCE CLAIMS PAID: REGISTER NOW

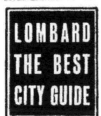

LOMBARD
THE BEST
CITY GUIDE

DailyMirror

THE DAILY PICTURE PAPER WITH THE LARGEST NET SALE

No. 7,977 | Registered at the G.P.O. as a Newspaper. | TUESDAY, JUNE 11, 1929 | One Penny

£100
CROSSWORD
PUZZLE

NEW CABINET MINISTERS MAKE A TALKIE

The new Cabinet before they made their talkie yesterday at 10, Downing-street. Left to right: (front) Mr. J. R. Clynes, Lord Parmoor, Mr. J. H. Thomas, Mr. Philip Snowden, Mr. Ramsay MacDonald, Mr. Arthur Henderson, Mr. Sidney Webb, Lord Justice Sankey, Captain Wedgwood Benn; (back) Mr. George Lansbury, Mr. A. V. Alexander, Sir C. P. Trevelyan, Miss Margaret Bondfield, Lord Thomson, Mr. Tom Shaw, Mr. Arthur Greenwood, Mr. Noel Buxton, Mr. W. Graham and Mr. W. Adamson.

Mr. J. H. Thomas (left) and Mr. George Lansbury going out to be filmed.

Mr. MacDonald receives directions from the camera-man.

Lord Parmoor and Miss Bondfield find the taking of the talkie a very funny business.

The new Cabinet are giving themselves a fresh introduction to the taxpayers by a talkie film, which was made yesterday in the garden of 10, Downing-street. All nineteen members of the Cabinet attended to join in this Ministerial novelty, and Mr. Ramsay Mac- Donald, speaking into a microphone, introduced each of his colleagues. He described Miss Bondfield as a " double first," she being the first woman Cabinet Minister and the first woman Privy Councillor. See also page 28.

62

MANY MORE INSURANCE CLAIMS PAID TO-DAY

£100 CROSSWORD PUZZLE

DailyMirror

THE DAILY PICTURE — PAPER WITH THE LARGEST NET SALE

No. 7,983 — Registered at the G.P.O. as a Newspaper — TUESDAY, JUNE 18, 1929 — One Penny

RACING CONTEST COUPON DAILY

SEVEN DEAD IN AIR DISASTER AT SEA

Wreckage of the great air liner City of Ottawa, which came down in the Channel yesterday, causing the deaths of seven persons, beside a rescuing vessel. All the dead were passengers, flying from London to Paris, and four passengers, as well as the pilot and mechanic, were injured, so that none of the occupants escaped unharmed. Six of the passengers were women. It is believed that the machine developed engine trouble, but before it hit the water the pilot reported his position. Several vessels rushed to the scene, and it is probably due to the pilot's message that total loss of all on board was avoided. See also pages 14 and 15.—("Daily Mirror" aerial photograph.)

GREAT NEW SERIAL BEGINS ON MONDAY

LOOK OUT FOR FRASS

DailyMirror

THE DAILY PICTURE PAPER WITH THE LARGEST NET SALE

No. 7,984 Registered at the G.P.O. as a Newspaper. WEDNESDAY, JUNE 19, 1929 One Penny

BEST FREE FAMILY INSURANCE

ROYALTY AT ASCOT'S SUNSHINE OPENING

Occupants of the Royal Box at Ascot yesterday, including the Duke of Connaught, Lady Patricia Ramsay and Princess Ingrid of Sweden. Princess Mary acted as hostess.

Old Orkney wins the Ascot Stakes from Brown Jack (hidden by winning post).

A striking ensemble. Full skirt and scarf are of the same material.

The Prince of Wales gazing keenly across the course from the royal box.

Princess Imeritinsky favoured the long skirt's return.

The one thing lacking from an otherwise perfect opening of Ascot was the royal procession, which, owing to the absence of the King and Queen, could not be held. In warmth and sunshine an immense crowd watched the racing, and the grace and beauty of the latest fashions were well illustrated. Parasols were few. All the big houses in the neighbourhood are in use for house parties. To-day's big race will be the Royal Hunt Cup. See also pages 14 and 15.—("Daily Mirror" photographs.)

THE DAILY MIRROR, Thursday, June 20, 1929.

DRAMATIC NEW SERIAL BEGINS ON MONDAY

FRASS AGAIN NEXT WEEK

DailyMirror

THE DAILY PICTURE PAPER WITH THE LARGEST NET SALE

LOMBARD THE BEST CITY GUIDE

No. 7,985 — Registered at the G.P.O. as a Newspaper. — THURSDAY, JUNE 20, 1929 — One Penny

STARTLING FASHION CONTRASTS AT ASCOT

A distinct contrast in fashions.

A long skirt style.

A long lace dress. The sun brought out many parasols yesterday.

Lace cloak with high collar.

On a coach top. Fur trimming was favoured by many women.

Above are illustrated some of the many startling dresses at Ascot yesterday. Freak and shapeless fashions, lacking neatness, have been a novel and striking feature of the paddock at this year's meeting. Skirts trailing behind their wearers, skirts full enough to billow out in the wind like crinolines, and skirts that are of ankle length have been seen side by side with curious creations reaching only to the knee. See also page 24.— ("Daily Mirror" photographs.)

65

£100 NEXT WEEK FOR FINDING FRASS

BEST FAMILY INSURANCE

DailyMirror

THE DAILY PICTURE ☙ PAPER WITH THE LARGEST NET SALE

No. 7,986 · Registered at the G.P.O. as a Newspaper. · FRIDAY, JUNE 21, 1929 · One Penny

NEW SERIAL ON MONDAY

FIRST PREMIER TO FLY—600 MILES TRIP

Miss Ishbel MacDonald helps to adjust the Prime Minister's parachute before his 600-mile flight yesterday from Lossiemouth to Hendon.—(By " Daily Mirror " photo-telephony.)

DEER-STALKING TRAGEDY INQUEST

Captain Lindsay Smith described how he accidentally shot dead Dr. Barbara Morris (right), while stalking a deer, in his evidence yesterday at the inquest at Hemel Hempstead, Hertfordshire. A verdict of Accidental death was returned.

Mr. MacDonald, the first British Prime Minister to fly, descending with his pilot, Flight-Lieutenant H. W. Heslop, R.A.F., from a Fairey bomber at Hendon yesterday. This is the Air Force's fastest two-seater, and the 'plane did the trip in flying time of 3h. 50m.

THE DAILY MIRROR, Monday, July 1, 1929.

BEST FAMILY INSURANCE: REGISTER TO-DAY

FRASS APPEARS TO-DAY

DailyMirror

THE DAILY PICTURE PAPER WITH THE LARGEST NET SALE

ANOTHER £1,000 PICTURE PUZZLE

No. 7,994   Registered at the G.P.C. as a Newspaper.   MONDAY, JULY 1, 1929   One Penny

ENGLAND'S NARROW DEFEAT IN GRAND PRIX

President Doumergue smiling down upon the crowd from the Presidential box.

The brilliant scene in front of the stand just before the race. All Paris Society was there.

The close finish of yesterday's Grand Prix, Hotweed just getting in front of Buland Bala. Calandria was third.

Wonderful dresses were seen at Longchamp yesterday. This picture illustrates the new floating veil.

The Aga Khan's Buland Bala, which was the only English horse in the race, was beaten in the Grand Prix at Longchamp yesterday by only the shortest of heads. Michael Beary was in the saddle and made a great effort. The winner was M. Esmond's Hotweed, the horse which won the French Derby a fortnight ago. There were twenty-three runners, which is a record field for this great race, the Blue Riband of the French Turf.—("Daily Mirror" photographs brought by air.)

LOOK OUT FOR FRASS: TO APPEAR TO-MORROW

MORE INSURANCE CLAIMS PAID

DailyMirror

THE DAILY PICTURE PAPER WITH THE LARGEST NET SALE

No. 7,995   Registered at the G.P.O. as a Newspaper.   TUESDAY, JULY 2, 1929   One Penny

RACING CONTEST FINAL COUPON

LONDON WELCOMES THE KING

Countless Thousands Express Empire's Joy at His Majesty's Return to Health

The King driving amid huge welcoming crowds in St. James's-street on his return yesterday to Buckingham Palace, whence, over four months ago, he was carried to Bognor in an ambulance. Inset, his Majesty bowing to the people. As he drove in the open landau with the Queen countless thousands of his Majesty's subjects, who "waited and watched" during his long illness, thronged the streets and declared with their loudest cheers the Empire's joy and thankfulness at his recovery of health. In a message issued from Buckingham Palace the King expressed "heartfelt gratitude" for his welcome. See also pages 12 and 13.—("Daily Mirror" photograph.)

FIND FRASS TO-DAY: CLUES ON PAGE 15

MORE INSURANCE CLAIMS PAID

DailyMirror

THE DAILY PICTURE PAPER WITH THE LARGEST NET SALE

No. 7,996 — Registered at the G.P.O. as a Newspaper. — WEDNESDAY, JULY 3, 1929 — One Penny

NEW £500 RACING CONTEST

NEW NATIONAL TRIBUTE TO SHAKESPEARE

A great crowd yesterday at the foundation stone-laying ceremony for the new Shakespeare Memorial Theatre at Stratford-on-Avon.

Lord Ampthill receiving a silver trowel from Miss Elizabeth Scott.

Miss Scott's architectural drawing of the new theatre.

Lord Ampthill using a level on the foundation stone after performing the laying ceremony.

Miss Scott, the architect, arriving.

The foundation-stone of the new Shakespeare Memorial Theatre at Stratford-on-Avon, which will replace the famous theatre that was burned in March, 1926, was laid yesterday by Lord Ampthill, pro-Grand Master of the United Grand Lodge of English Freemasons, at the formal request of Lord Burnham, president of the Theatre Governors. Miss Elizabeth Scott, the young architect of the new theatre, took a prominent part in the proceedings.—("Daily Mirror" photographs.)

69

HOW FRASS WAS FOUND IN THE SEA

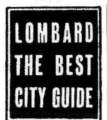

LOMBARD THE BEST CITY GUIDE

DailyMirror

THE DAILY PICTURE PAPER WITH THE LARGEST NET SALE

No. 7,997   Registered at the G.P.O. as a Newspaper   THURSDAY, JULY 4, 1929   One Penny

£1,000 PICTURE PUZZLE WEEKLY

BRILLIANT OPENING DAY FOR ROYAL HENLEY

...y 'Margate' (Cambridge) defeating New College (Oxford) in the second heat of the Ladies' Plate by 1¼ lengths at Henley, where the regatta opened yesterday.

Lord Tiverton, Diamond Sculls competitor

Columbia University, U.S.A., after winning a Thames Challenge Cup heat.

River girls have refreshments between races.

Summer made a welcome reappearance for the opening of the famous regatta at Henley yesterday, and a meeting distinguished by the presence of transatlantic crews had a most auspicious start. These include Argonaut, one of the strongest Canadian clubs, and

Columbia University, U.S.A. Another interesting entry is that of Viscount Tiverton, son of Lord Halsbury, in the Diamond Sculls. He won his heat against H. P. Murdoch by five lengths. A great many river craft of all kinds lined the course. See also page 15.

THE DAILY MIRROR, Friday, July 5, 1929

£1,000 FOR A PICTURE PUZZLE SOLUTION

BEST FREE FAMILY INSURANCE

DailyMirror

THE DAILY PICTURE PAPER WITH THE LARGEST NET SALE

No. 7,998   Registered at the G.P.O. as a Newspaper.   FRIDAY, JULY 5, 1929   One Penny

FRASS APPEARS TO-DAY

WOMEN PILOTS IN RECORD KING'S CUP RACE

Miss W. E. Spooner.

Mrs. A. S. Butler.

Lady Bailey.

Captain W. L. Hope.

Competitors' 'planes at Heston Aerodrome yesterday, when all taking part in the race had to report.

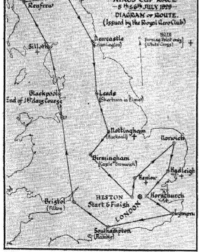

A diagram of the two-days course.

Lady Bailey studies the map.

Miss Spooner looking at a Gloster "Grebe," a speedy competing 'plane.

To-day and to-morrow will be flown the eighth air race for the famous King's Cup, the entry of forty-two being a record one. Three women will compete: Lady Bailey, who flew alone to South Africa and back; Miss Spooner, who put up a magnificent fight last year and finished third; and Mrs. A. S. Butler, whose husband is also an entrant. Captain W. L. Hope will try to do the hat trick, having won in 1927 and 1928. The machines will follow a 1,169 miles circuit of England.

THE KING X-RAYED: NORFOLK VISIT POSTPONED

MORE INSURANCE CLAIMS PAID

DailyMirror

THE DAILY PICTURE PAPER WITH THE LARGEST NET SALE

No. 8,001   Registered at the G.P.O. as a Newspaper.   TUESDAY, JULY 9, 1929   One Penny

FRASS: £100 REWARD TO-DAY

FIRST LORD'S VISIT TO GIANT BATTLESHIP

The review of H.M.S. Nelson's crew by Mr. A. V. Alexander.

Mr. A. V. Alexander making a tour of Nelson preceded by Captain T. H. Binney, D.S.O

An inspection of a 6in. gun in H.M.S. Nelson, one of the largest battleships, by Mr. A. V. Alexander, First Lord of the Admiralty, during his visit yesterday to Torbay.

U.S. TO ROME FLIGHT ATTEMPT

Captain Lewis Yancey (taller) and Mr. Roger Williams, Americans, who started yesterday in their aeroplane, the Pathfinder, on an attempted flight from Old Orchard, Maine, to Rome. They made unsuccessful bids in the Green Flash.

MINERS LOST IN BLAZING PIT DISASTER

£1,000 PICTURE PUZZLE WEEKLY

DailyMirror

THE DAILY PICTURE PAPER WITH THE LARGEST NET SALE

No. 8,003   Registered at the G.P.O. as a Newspaper.   THURSDAY, JULY 11, 1929   One Penny

FRASS APPEARS TO-DAY

AIR LEVIATHANS—END OF RECORD FLIGHT

The huge German all-steel flying-ship Dox, which may revolutionise aviation, lying in its shed at Friedrichshafen. Measuring 150ft. in length and 150ft. from wing tip to wing tip, it is equipped with twelve engines of 500 horse-power and is intended to carry 100 passengers. It will have two pilots, instructed by a captain, and a navigator. Mechanics will be able to reach the engines from inside each wing. The craft is to be launched on Lake Constance to-day.

The Southern Cross landing at Croydon yesterday from Australia and—right—her gallant crew immediately after arrival. (A to B) Flight-Lieutenant McWilliam, wireless operator; Flight-Lieutenant Ulm, navigator; Captain Kingsford Smith, pilot; and Flight-Lieutenant Litchfield. The flight was completed in less than thirteen days, breaking Bert Hinkler's record. Captain Kingsford Smith and Flight-Lieutenant Ulm had already crossed the Pacific from America to Australia in the same machine.

HOW M. LEROUX LANDED ON "HIS" ISLAND

FRASS APPEARS TO-MORROW

Daily Mirror

THE DAILY PICTURE PAPER WITH THE LARGEST NET SALE

No. 8,006 — Registered at the G.P.O. as a Newspaper. — MONDAY, JULY 15, 1929 — One Penny

SPECIAL EDITION

ITALY'S NARROW WIN IN IRISH GRAND PRIX

Drivers rush to their cars at the start of the great race.

The Italian Ivanowsky in his Alfa Romeo crossing the winning line.

President Cosgrave presents the handsome Phœnix Trophy to the winner.

First and second congratulate each other after the race. Kidston has his hand on Ivanowsky's shoulder.

G. E. T. Eyston helps to put out a fire in the Bugatti he was driving. He had to retire.

Thrills abounded in the Grand Prix motor race, which was watched by 100,000 people, at Phœnix Park, Dublin, on Saturday. Four nations competed, and though Britain was unable to obtain first place, the greatness of her fight can be judged from the fact that she took the next three. Ivanowsky (Alfa Romeo), was first, 14s. ahead of G. Kidston (Bentley). H. R. S. Birkin and B. H. Wood (both Bentley) were third and fourth respectively. See also page 28.—("Daily Mirror.")

STOP THE MOUNTING TOLL OF THE ROADS

MOTOR ARTICLE TO-DAY

DailyMirror

THE DAILY PICTURE PAPER WITH THE LARGEST NET SALE

No. 8,010 Registered at the G.P.O. as a Newspaper. FRIDAY, JULY 19, 1929 One Penny

WHAT TO HEAR ON THE GRAMOPHONE

BRITAIN THREATENED WITH A REAL DROUGHT

Their pond having dried up, these cottagers near Wallingford have to go half-a-mile for water.

Water is " on " for only four hours in 48 at Steventon, Berkshire.

This rather muddy brook is one resource for water-famined people at Steventon.

Though the water-shortage is most severely felt in the north, the prospect of continued dry weather now seriously threatens the south of England. Already at Steventon, Berkshire, there is a supply only every other day. London, however, is in a comparatively favourable position, though two Thames tributaries have dried up.

BRITON CHARGED WITH PARIS MURDER

Sidney Harle in custody of a policeman in Paris, where he is charged with the murder of a four-year-old French girl whose body was found in a trunk. He is a native of Newbury, Berkshire. He says that he accidentally ran her down with his cycle. See news page.—(Picture by " Daily Mirror " photo-telephony.)

THE DAILY MIRROR, Wednesday, July 31, 1929.

NEW MOTORING REGULATIONS TO-MORROW

FRASS APPEARS AGAIN TO-MORROW

DailyMirror

THE DAILY PICTURE PAPER WITH THE LARGEST NET SALE

No. 8,020 | Registered at the G.P.O. as a Newspaper. | WEDNESDAY, JULY 31, 1929 | One Penny

BEST FAMILY HOLIDAY INSURANCE

A GLORIOUS WIN AT GLORIOUS GOODWOOD

Viscountess Hood and Miss Rosemary Hood at Goodwood yesterday.

Around the table (left to right), Mrs. Davey, Mrs. Russell, Mrs. du Cros, Mrs. Longworth, General McDonall, Major du Cros, Major Little, Mr. Priestley and Captain Russell at a Goodwood luncheon party.

Baroness Zouche's cheerful luncheon party in the car park

Mr. S. B. Joel's Fleeting Memory winning the Stewards' Cup from Golden Oracle and Dark Fire.

The great crowd which for the first time paid to watch the racing from Trundle Hill, a natural grandstand 600ft. high. This is now enclosed by railings (seen in background) and an admission fee of 3s. is charged. Higher taxation and increased expenses of up-keep have necessitated this, it is explained on behalf of the Duke of Richmond. Bouverie, the " Daily Mirror's " racing expert, napped Fleeting Memory, and it won at 100 to 8, although badly kicked at the start. See also page 11.

THE DAILY MIRROR, Thursday, August 1, 1929.

£50 REWARD FOR FINDING FRASS TO-DAY

£1,500 IN PRIZES

DailyMirror

THE DAILY PICTURE PAPER WITH THE LARGEST NET SALE

No. 8,021 | Registered at the G.P.O. as a Newspaper. | THURSDAY, AUGUST 1, 1929 | One Penny

BEST HOLIDAY INSURANCE

REDS HANDCUFFED TO BUS

Police officers removing from the top of an L.G.O.C. No. 29a bus a woman, one of a Communist party of three women and a man, who handcuffed themselves to the seats and had a banner inscribed, "Workers, strike against war preparations—August 1."

Four other Communist women got on the bus and sang the "Red Flag." The bus was driven to Cannon-row Station, the whole party was taken into custody and the handcuffed four marched into the police station singing. See also page 24.

£1,000 PICTURE PUZZLE EVERY WEEK: SEE P. 17

FRASS APPEARS TO-DAY

DailyMirror

THE DAILY PICTURE PAPER WITH THE LARGEST NET SALE

No. 8,023   Registered at the G.P.O. as a Newspaper.   **SATURDAY, AUGUST 3, 1929**   One Penny

BEST HOLIDAY INSURANCE

HOLIDAY CALL IS THE LOUDEST OF ALL!

Starting for the West from Paddington yesterday.

The loud call of holiday that thousands answer.

Holiday 'planes were triplicated at Croydon yesterday.

The seaside is Britain's playground during August. If only the weather will be kind, this is likely to be the greatest holiday for years.

The great rush to the south coast at Waterloo yesterday. Most of the travellers heeded the Air Ministry's caution that umbrellas or mackintoshes were advisable companions. The misgivings of the weather experts provide the only doubtful aspect of this great summer holiday. But undismayed crowds packed the London railway termini yesterday and found a new form of holiday travel by combined rail, road, river and sea trips. On the other hand, bigger crowds than ever went to the Continent by air.

GREAT NEW SERIAL "STORM BIRD" TO-MORROW

FILM NOTES TO-DAY

DailyMirror

THE DAILY PICTURE PAPER WITH THE LARGEST NET SALE

No. 8,026   Registered at the G.P.O. as a Newspaper   WEDNESDAY, AUGUST 7, 1929   One Penny

BEST HOLIDAY INSURANCE

CRANE'S CRASH ON TRAMCAR

APPOINTMENT

The scene of the crane accident in Glasgow yesterday. A crane weighing over a ton crashed on the top of a tramcar, ripping open the roof. Five passengers and four pedestrians were injured and taken to hospital.—(By " Daily Mirror " photo-telephony.)

MURDER VERDICT IN ARSENIC CASE

Dr. H. B. Jackson.   Mr. E. C. Duff.   Mrs. Duff.

A verdict that Mr. Edmund Creighton Duff's death was due to acute arsenical poisoning and that he was murdered by some person or persons unknown was returned at the resumed inquest conducted at Croydon yesterday by Dr. H. B. Jackson.

Sir Percy Loraine, British Minister in Athens, whose appointment to succeed Lord Lloyd, late High Commissioner in Egypt, was announced yesterday by the Cairo newspaper " El Ahram." Lord Lloyd's resignation a fortnight ago caused a political sensation and was the subject of discussions in both Houses of Parliament.

BEGIN OUR NEW SERIAL, "STORM BIRD," TO-DAY

RACING CONTEST RESULT ON PAGE 2

DailyMirror

THE DAILY PICTURE   PAPER WITH THE LARGEST NET SALE

No. 8,028   Registered at the G.P.O. as a Newspaper.   FRIDAY, AUGUST 9, 1929   One Penny

BEST HOLIDAY INSURANCE

HUMOURS OF THE LITTLE "WAR" IN SUSSEX

A one-man arsenal walking ashore on a Sussex beach.

A Grey soldier who apparently would prefer to fight on land. Salt water is very fatiguing.

Downland troops, rushed up from Worthing by motor-coach, charging into a smoke-screen on Hill 400.

Troops landing while others are hauling in the cutters which brought them from the ships H.M.S. Iron Duke and Tribune dimly seen in the distance.

Thousands of holidaymakers lined the cliffs between Peacehaven and Brighton yesterday to watch the conclusion of the "war" on the Sussex coast. They saw, however, little of the movement of troops, but were thrilled by the heavy fire which the battleship Iron Duke, a Greyland unit, poured into the Downland positions after the soldiers and sailors had landed. These came ashore with boots and socks hung round their necks and forming up on the beach marched to the downs.—("Daily Mirror" photographs.)

BEST HOLIDAY INSURANCE: REGISTER TO-DAY

LOOK OUT FOR FRASS TO-MORROW

DailyMirror

THE DAILY PICTURE PAPER WITH THE LARGEST NET SALE

No. 8,030   Registered at the G.P.O. as a Newspaper.   MONDAY, AUGUST 12, 1929   One Penny

NEW £1,000 PICTURE PUZZLE

BRITISH LEGION SALUTE FOR HAIG'S DAUGHTER

The British Legion guard of honour cheering the bride at the church door after the marriage of Mr. Andrew Montagu-Douglas-Scott and Lady Victoria Haig, daughter of the late Field-Marshal Earl Haig, at Mertoun, near Bemersyde.

LOST GIRL FOUND

Hilda Harvey, aged six, who disappeared when playing in the street near her home at Manor Park, E. She was found the next day near Romford, Essex, in the company of a strange man.

The bride and bridegroom beside the ancient sundial at Bemersyde.

SCOUT'S BRAVERY

Andre Begaert, a Belgian scout, aged fourteen, who saved three companions endangered by broken ice last winter, has been awarded a medal by the King of the Belgians. He attended the jamboree.

MANY INSURANCE CLAIMS PAID: REGISTER NOW

FRASS APPEARS TO-DAY

DailyMirror

THE DAILY PICTURE ● PAPER WITH THE LARGEST NET SALE

No 8,031 | Registered at the G.P.O as a Newspaper | TUESDAY, AUGUST 13, 1929 | One Penny

£100 CROSSWORD PUZZLE

BRITAIN'S 360 M.P.H. SCHNEIDER TROPHY RACER

The new Supermarine Rolls-Royce S 6, the principal British " hope " for next month's Schneider Trophy race, at Calshot yesterday. Its speed is given as 360 m.p.h.

The S 6 being towed out to sea. The pilot was Squadron-Leader A. H. Orlebar, the captain of the Schneider Trophy team.—(" Daily Mirror.")

No one knows the capabilities of Britain's new Supermarine Rolls-Royce S 6, a demonstration of which was given at Calshot yesterday, but a possible speed of 400 m.p.h. has been hinted at. It is obviously a vastly superior seaplane to that which won the last Schneider Trophy race. It has a new and secret type of engine, larger and more powerful, and its stream lining is a revelation. Another novel feature is that the fuel is carried in the floats. Many of the machines' secrets are closely guarded.

THE DAILY MIRROR, Monday, August 19, 1929.

BEST HOLIDAY INSURANCE: REGISTER TO-DAY

FRASS APPEARS AGAIN TO-MORROW

DailyMirror

THE DAILY PICTURE ◆ PAPER WITH THE LARGEST NET SALE

NEW £1,000 PICTURE PUZZLE

No. 8,036 — Registered at the G.P.O. as a Newspaper. — MONDAY, AUGUST 19, 1929 — One Penny

EXCITING INCIDENTS IN THE GREAT ROAD RACE

The Duke of Abercorn, Governor of Northern Ireland, giving the winner his laurel.

The Aston Martin driven by P. H. Turnbull being pushed back to the road.

Competitors passing a large crowd when taking a corner at Newtownards.

R. Carraciola, the winner, at the finishing line in his Mercedes Benz.

Cars bunched together in rounding Quarry Corner. No. 22 is Kaye Don's Lea Francis.—("Daily Mirror" photographs.)

In winning the great race for the R.A.C. Tourist Trophy at Belfast, R. Carraciola, a German competitor, gave a superb exhibition of driving with amazing speed and cornering throughout the 410-mile course. He paid tribute, however, to the Austins, and said that although it was a great moment when he passed C. Campari, who was second in an Alfa Romeo, it was a greater one when he got ahead of the little British cars, The winner's time was 5h. 32m. 40s. and average speed 72.82 m.p.h.

MANY INSURANCE CLAIMS PAID: REGISTER NOW

£100 CROSSWORD PUZZLE

DailyMirror

THE DAILY PICTURE PAPER WITH THE LARGEST NET SALE

No. 8,037 | Registered at the G.P.O. as a Newspaper. | TUESDAY, AUGUST 20, 1929 | One Penny

FRASS APPEARS TO-DAY

GIRLS' 30,000-MILE FEAT

Miss Violet Cordery (at the wheel) and Miss Evelyn Cordery, her sister, after completing yesterday the feat of driving 30,000 miles at over 60 m.p.h. at Brooklands. They started on June 18 and took turns at the wheel almost daily.

EX-ARCHDEACON'S WIFE REVIVES OLD CRAFT

Mrs. Wakeford, wife of ex-Archdeacon John Wakeford, in her newly-opened workshop at Pole Steeple, Biggin Hill, Kent, where she has revived the craft of rush chair-making. Specially-grown rushes are used for the work.

ATLANTIC FLYERS

M. Oscar Kaeser (dark suit), pilot, and M. Luescher, mechanic, who left Lisbon yesterday with M. Tschopp, navigator, to fly to New York. They intended to pass over the Azores.

AMES'S "DUCK" IN HIS FIRST TEST

Ames caught by Mitchell off McMillan's bowling in the Test match against South Africa at the Oval yesterday. It was his first Test match and he scored a "duck." England were all out for 258.

THE DAILY MIRROR, Tuesday, August 27, 1929

MANY INSURANCE CLAIMS PAID: REGISTER NOW

£100 CROSSWORD PUZZLE

Daily Mirror

THE DAILY PICTURE PAPER WITH THE LARGEST NET SALE

LOMBARD THE BEST CITY GUIDE

No. 8,043 | Registered at the G.P.O. as a Newspaper. | TUESDAY, AUGUST 27, 1929 | One Penny

NIGHT WORK ON BRITISH SCHNEIDER RACER

Working by searchlight at Calshot on the S 6, under the eye of an armed guard. Mr. R. J. Mitchell, the designer, looks on from the ground.

Italian pilots among the spectators watching flying from a tower.

Like a giant dragonfly—the front view of the Italian 'plane Superbo.

Although no official intimation has been received whether Italy will withdraw from the Schneider Trophy contest, preparations at Calshot are being pushed forward in both the British and the Italian advance guard camps. Lieutenant-Commander H. Perrin, secre-tary of the Royal Aero Club, states that the race will take place even in the absence of the Italians. The only American challenger, Lieutenant Williams, failed to rise in his machine at Annapolis, Maryland, and will not compete.—(" Daily Mirror " photographs.)

GERMANY ACCEPTS PROPOSALS AT THE HAGUE

£1,000 PICTURE PUZZLE WEEKLY

Daily Mirror

THE DAILY PICTURE PAPER WITH THE LARGEST NET SALE

No. 8,046   Registered at the G.P.O. as a Newspaper   FRIDAY, AUGUST 30, 1929   One Penny

BEST HOLIDAY INSURANCE

HISTORIC CASTLE DESTROYED BY FIRE

A photograph taken from a "Daily Mirror" aeroplane of Lulworth Castle, one of the most historic buildings in Dorset, on fire yesterday. After being ablaze for many hours the castle was reduced to a shell, the water supply giving out when the flames had almost been got under control. Two firemen were badly burned when a deluge of molten lead fell from the roof. Many villagers, men from the Tank Corps School and girl guides saved valuable furniture, pictures and antiques and some of these are seen above piled upon the lawn. The foundation of Lulworth Castle was laid in 1588. Seven Kings of England have stayed there. See also pages 12 and 13.

"THE GLORIOUS HUNDRED DAYS": BY VISCOUNT ROTHERMERE

NEW £1,000 PICTURE PUZZLE

Daily Mirror

THE DAILY PICTURE PAPER WITH THE LARGEST NET SALE

No. 8,048 — Registered at the G.P.O. as a Newspaper. — MONDAY, SEPTEMBER 2, 1929 — One Penny

BEST HOLIDAY INSURANCE

THE KING WALKING HOME AFTER SERVICE

The King and Queen walking from Sandringham Parish Church to Sandringham House yesterday morning after attending service. The King was looking much better.

LONDON'S GREAT WELCOME TO THE CHANCELLOR AFTER HIS REPARATIONS TRIUMPH

Mr. and Mrs. Snowden at Liverpool-street yesterday, when they were cheered by a crowd of 5,000 people on their return from the Chancellor's triumph at The Hague. | Right, some of the great crowd thronging the station. Communists attempting to distribute leaflets attacking Mr. Snowden were roughly handled.—("Daily Mirror.")

MANY INSURANCE CLAIMS PAID: REGISTER NOW

£100 CROSSWORD PUZZLE

DailyMirror

THE DAILY PICTURE PAPER WITH THE LARGEST NET SALE

LOMBARD THE BEST CITY GUIDE

No. 8,049   Registered at the G.P.O. as a Newspaper   TUESDAY, SEPTEMBER 3, 1929   One Penny

MANY DEATHS IN SHOP FIRE DISASTER

Firemen playing a hose on burning shops during a great fire in which eleven people lost their lives at Rolfe-street, Smethwick, near Birmingham, early yesterday. The victims belong to three families who were trapped by flames while asleep. They are Mr. and Mrs. MacDonald and their four young children, Mr. and Mrs. James Jones and their son, and Mrs. Mary Aston and her son. Ena Jones, aged twenty-three, and Emily and Lilian Aston, aged twenty-three and fifteen respectively, jumped from third story windows and were seriously injured. Others escaped in their night clothes. The Theatre Royal was also involved in the outbreak, first noticed by a booking clerk at the L.M.S. station.

THE DAILY MIRROR, Wednesday, September 4, 1929.

PREMIER'S SPEECH AT THE LEAGUE OF NATIONS

£1,000
PICTURE
PUZZLE
WEEKLY

DailyMirror

THE DAILY PICTURE PAPER WITH THE LARGEST NET SALE

No. 8,050   Registered at the G.P.O. as a Newspaper   WEDNESDAY, SEPTEMBER 4, 1929   One Penny

BEST
HOLIDAY
INSURANCE

PRINCE OF WALES WITH HIGH-SPEED PILOTS

The Prince of Wales with the Italian Schneider Trophy pilots whom he met at Calshot yesterday after flying from Brooklands. He also met the British pilots

Wives of British Schneider Trophy pilots watching a practice flight. A to B Mrs. Stainforth, Mrs. Moon, Mrs. Orlebar, wife of the captain, and Mrs. Waghorn.

Watching the Gloucester-Napier machine flashing past in the sky.

The Prince of Wales flew to Calshot yesterday on a surprise visit to both teams engaging on Saturday in the great Schneider Trophy high-speed air race. In the Italian hangar he saw the famous egg-shaped Fiat, said to be the smallest fast seaplane in the world. His instant comment was: "Isn't she a beauty? I would love to have a flip in her." Previously the Prince had flown round the course in a Royal Air Force flying-boat.—("Daily Mirror" photographs.)

LONDON GIRL SHOT DEAD ON HONEYMOON

£500 RACING CONTEST RESULT

DailyMirror

THE DAILY PICTURE PAPER WITH THE LARGEST NET SALE

SPECIAL EDITION

No. 8,051   Registered at the G.P.O. as a Newspaper.   THURSDAY, SEPTEMBER 5, 1929   One Penny

SHOT DEAD   HOTTEST SEPTEMBER FOR YEARS

Mrs. Irma Wigget, the Englishwoman who was found shot dead in a big hotel in Paris. A warrant has been issued for the arrest of her husband, Edgar Wigget. Watch is kept at French ports and frontiers for him.

WRESTLING PRINCE

Sir Herbert Barker, the well-known bonesetter, and the Maharaj Kumar of Kutch, engaged in a wrestling match on the lawn of La Moye Manor, a house that was once a monastery, in Jersey.

Fashions in the pleasure gardens at Folkestone reminiscent of the Lido and eminently suitable for the September heat wave which was at its height yesterday. The shade temperature of 87 deg. at 4 p.m. in London equalled the previous record for that date reached on September 4, 1880.

END OF ZEPPELIN'S 20 DAYS ROUND THE WORLD TRIP

The Graf Zeppelin at Friedrichshafen yesterday morning when she returned to her base at the completion of her marvellous flight round the world in just over twenty days. She was escorted by a dozen aeroplanes and her crew were greeted with wild enthusiasm.—(By " Daily Mirror " photo-telephony from Berlin.)

BEST HOLIDAY INSURANCE: REGISTER TO-DAY

LAUGH DAILY WITH THE PATER

DailyMirror

THE DAILY PICTURE PAPER WITH THE LARGEST NET SALE

SPECIAL EDITION

No. 8,053   Registered at the G.P.O. as a Newspaper.   SATURDAY, SEPTEMBER 7, 1929   One Penny

1913-1929: SCHNEIDER SPEED CONTRASTS

The amazing progress that has been made in air speeds since the first Schneider Trophy race in 1913 is graphically illustrated above. In that year the winner averaged 45.75 m.p.h., a speed which would have taken him from London to Brighton or Colchester in one hour. Seaplanes of the type which are competing to-day have achieved speeds in the neighbourhood of 360 m.p.h., and in direct flight at top speed they could reach Edinburgh or Dublin from London in about an hour. Inset above, a Supermarine Rolls-Royce S 6, entered for the race; below, the Deperdussin which won in 1913. See also page 20.—(Relief model map by courtesy of George Philip and Son, Ltd.)

MANY INSURANCE CLAIMS PAID: REGISTER NOW

£1,000 PICTURE PUZZLE WEEKLY

DailyMirror

THE DAILY PICTURE — PAPER WITH THE LARGEST NET SALE

No. 8,055   Registered at the G.P.O. as a Newspaper.   TUESDAY, SEPTEMBER 10, 1929   One Penny

LOMBARD THE BEST CITY GUIDE

FIRST PICTURES OF PALESTINE OUTRAGES

The shell of a Jewish house which was set on fire by Arabs at Bikor Hayeem when the anti-Jewish riots, marked by incendiarism, looting and fighting, were at their height. British troops, rushed into the country by ship and aeroplane, have since been able to re-establish order.

FIFTEEN MEN DEAD IN BRITISH OIL TANKER BLAZE

Pillaged home at Talpioth, a suburb of Jerusalem.

The British oil tanker Vimeira, which caught fire at Rotterdam. Fifteen men are believed to have lost their lives, having either jumped overboard or been trapped by the flames. The vessel was bound for Glasgow. The captain's wife, Mrs. Eva Finlayson, jumped from the wheelhouse and broke a leg.

Sir John Chancellor, the High Commissioner, inspects members of Wycliffe Hall, Oxford, who rendered great help to the authorities. These exclusive " Daily Mirror " pictures are the first that show the actual results of the serious outbreaks, in which many were killed. See also page 24.

THE DAILY MIRROR, Wednesday, September 11, 1929

£1,200 PICTURE PUZZLE FOR REGISTERED READERS

LAUGH DAILY WITH THE PATER

Daily Mirror

THE DAILY PICTURE PAPER WITH THE LARGEST NET SALE

No. 8,056   Registered at the G.P.O. as a Newspaper.   WEDNESDAY, SEPTEMBER 11, 1929   One Penny

BEST FAMILY INSURANCE

AIR RECORD OF 355.8 M.P.H. WON FOR BRITAIN

Squadron-Leader Orlebar being carried ashore from the Supermarine Rolls-Royce S 6 after his record flight at 355.8 m.p.h.

The Supermarine Rolls-Royce S 6, piloted by Squadron-Leader Orlebar, during the flight.

Flight-Lieutenant Stainforth (x) returning after his great flight.

Spectators on Calshot Tower see the Gloster-Napier 6 pass on the last lap.

The world speed record, held by Italy, was beaten yesterday by over 37 m.p.h. by Squadron-Leader A. H. Orlebar, A.F.C., in the Supermarine Rolls-Royce S 6 which won the Schneider Trophy. Flying from Calshot he attained an average of 355.8 m.p.h., one lap being done at 368.8 m.p.h. Flight-Lieutenant G. H. Stainforth reached 351.3 m.p.h. in a Gloster-Napier 6 and had an average of 336.3 m.p.h. Visibility was poor, and Squadron-Leader Orlebar will try, to-morrow if possible, to beat his record.

DRAMATIC NEW SERIAL BEGINS NEXT MONDAY

£1,000 PICTURE PUZZLE WEEKLY

Daily Mirror

THE DAILY PICTURE PAPER WITH THE LARGEST NET SALE

No. 8,057   Registered at the G.P.O as a Newspaper.   THURSDAY, SEPTEMBER 12, 1929   One Penny

LOMBARD THE BEST CITY GUIDE

DERBY WINNER'S VICTORY IN THE ST. LEGER

The finish of the St. Leger at Doncaster yesterday. Trigo, winner of this year's Derby, won by a short head. Inset, Michael Beary, Trigo's jockey, after the race.

An aerial picture of the St. Leger course. Inset, Miss Anderson, of Mitcheldean, Gloucestershire, who drew Trigo in the Royal Calcutta Turf Club Sweepstakes and won £16,000.

Mr. R. C. Dawson (in light hat), trainer of Trigo, and Mr. W. Barnett, its owner. Mr. Barnett is a Belfast corn merchant.

Mr. W. Barnett, the owner of Trigo, yesterday's St. Leger winner, is what is known as a "small" owner and has bred and raced horses chiefly in Ireland. The only horse besides Trigo he has in England is Trigo's brother, Athford, which has won the Newbury Spring Cup and the Kempton Park Jubilee Handicap. In yesterday's race Lord Derby's Bosworth was second and Sir Laurence Philipps's Horus third, three-quarters of a length from Bosworth It was a splendid and thrilling finish

94

NEW SERIAL, "MYSTERY OF FLEET HALL," ON MONDAY

£10,000 ACCIDENT INSURANCE

Daily Mirror
THE DAILY PICTURE PAPER WITH THE LARGEST NET SALE

No. 8,059 — Registered at the G.P.O as a Newspaper. — SATURDAY, SEPTEMBER 14, 1929 — One Penny

SPECIAL EDITION

"DAILY MIRROR" TROPHY WON BY SCOTLAND

W. Drummond, the winner in his Gang Warily during the last lap.

The Mayor, Mr A Evans, presenting the "Daily Mirror" trophy to J. W. Drummond.

No 418 Peespeed II, driven by P G Dinsdale the owner going all out

Competitors dashing round the course. Only five of the twenty-three starters finished. Blue Peter IV. sank. Mr. P. Godfrey jumped into a patrol boat.

The " Daily Mirror " £50 international challenge trophy for " B " class outboard motor boats and cheque for £100 were won easily at Lowestoft yesterday by J. W. Drummond, his time being 2h. 4m. 23s. for the course of 50 nautical miles and his average speed over 25 m.p.h. The winner qualified in the eliminating trial at Glasgow and his fine victory was the result of a really great battle. Mishaps to several of the boats led to narrow escapes. See also page 20.

THE DAILY MIRROR, Wednesday, September 25, 1929.

£20 GIFT OF WIRELESS APPARATUS EVERY DAY

£1,000 PICTURE PUZZLE WEEKLY

Daily Mirror

THE DAILY PICTURE PAPER WITH THE LARGEST NET SALE

LOMBARD THE BEST CITY GUIDE

No. 8,068   Registered at the G.P.O. as a Newspaper.   WEDNESDAY, SEPTEMBER 25, 1929   One Penny

RHINELAND EVACUATED BY 300 ARMY PETS

Happy Tommies with their pets on arrival at Dover yesterday from the Rhine. Nearly 300 cats and dogs were members of this evacuation party.

THE PRINCE'S WIN AT R.A.F. GOLF MEETING

The Prince of Wales who, as a Group Captain, won the nine holes second division handicap with a return of 45—6, 39, at the championship meeting of the R.A.F. Golf Association at Sunningdale yesterday. The Duke of York has been elected Captain of the Royal and Ancient at St. Andrews for next year.

"We belong to the British Army, too." Special arrangements were made for the transport of the animals and their reception in England, including accommodation during the six months period of quarantine which is compulsory.

NEW £500 MUST-BE-WON PUZZLE PRIZE

£1,500 IN PRIZES

DailyMirror

THE DAILY PICTURE PAPER WITH THE LARGEST NET SALE

No. 8,078   Registered at the G.P.O. as a Newspaper.   MONDAY, OCTOBER 7, 1929   One Penny

32 PAGES

WINTER FASHIONS

MEMORIES OF SALONIKA

Field-Marshal Sir George Milne inspecting nurses who were at Salonika.

The Chaplain General to the Forces, the Rev. A. C. E. Jarvis, conducting the service.

An evening wrap of heavy honey-coloured satin with pompadour pink lining and trimming of beige dyed fox fur. Other pictures of the winter fashions are on pages 16 and 17. Baroque.—("Daily Mirror" photograph.)

Men and women to the number of 2,500 who served at Salonika were inspected by Field-Marshal Sir George Milne on the Horse Guards Parade yesterday, the eleventh anniversary of the signing of the armistice with Bulgaria.—("Daily Mirror" photographs.)

MANY INSURANCE CLAIMS PAID: REGISTER NOW

£500
MUST-BE-WON
**PUZZLE
PRIZE**

Daily Mirror

THE DAILY PICTURE PAPER WITH THE LARGEST NET SALE

No. 8,085   Registered at the G.P.O. as a Newspaper.   TUESDAY, OCTOBER 15, 1929   One Penny

**LOMBARD
THE BEST
CITY GUIDE**

R 101'S MAIDEN FLIGHT OVER LONDON

The new British airship R 101, the largest in the world, photographed on her maiden flight over London yesterday from an aeroplane above her stern. Among easily recognisable landmarks are Blackfriars Bridge—at the bottom of the picture—St. Paul's Cathedral and Southwark Bridge. Millions of people had a magnificent view of the air giant on the route from her base at Cardington to the metropolis and back. She flew over Bedford, Leighton Buzzard, Luton, and St. Albans. The crew numbered thirty-eight and there were fourteen passengers. Major Scott, the commander, stated after the test that the craft proved more easy to handle than expected.

A BETTER MOTOR SHOW THAN EVER THIS YEAR

LAUGH DAILY WITH THE PATER

DailyMirror

THE DAILY PICTURE • PAPER WITH THE LARGEST NET SALE

No. 8,086 Registered at the G.P.O. as a Newspaper. WEDNESDAY, OCTOBER 16, 1929 One Penny

BEST FAMILY INSURANCE

NO OFFICIAL EXISTENCE

Mr. James Mead, of Southsea, a twin who has no official existence, his birth registration having been omitted. He does not know if his name is James or John.

EX-PREMIER DIES

M. Delacroix, former Belgian Prime Minister, who suddenly died yesterday at Baden-Baden, Germany, where he was a delegate to the conference on the Bank of International Settlements.

STEAMER BLOWS UP AND SINKS

The French steamer Oklahoma in flames and sinking in Sandon Dock, Liverpool, yesterday. Explosions hurled wreckage far and wide.

HIGH COMMISSIONER'S DAUGHTER WED

Professor T. A. Smiddy (left), High Commissioner for the Irish Free State, with the bride and bridegroom after the wedding of his daughter, Miss C. Smiddy, and Commissioner Kevin O'Sheil at the Brompton Oratory yesterday.

Firemen pouring water into the blazing vessel. Two were injured and a passenger in a passing train was hurt by a flying piece of wreckage. Neighbouring vessels caught alight but these outbreaks were quelled.—(By " Daily Mirror " photo-telephony.)

PENSIONS FOR 500,000 MORE WIDOWS: PAGE 3

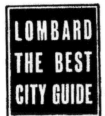

LOMBARD THE BEST CITY GUIDE

DailyMirror

THE DAILY PICTURE PAPER WITH THE LARGEST NET SALE

No. 8,087 — Registered at the G.P.O. as a Newspaper. — THURSDAY, OCTOBER 17, 1929 — One Penny

FIRST MOTOR SHOW NUMBER

TO-DAY'S GREAT MOTOR SHOW AT OLYMPIA

A luxury car with a table and receptacles for glasses and refreshments.

The show's cheapest British six-cylinder saloon car—a 16 h.p. Singer.

A camping car which has two convertible beds inside and carries a tent.

A temporary glass panel shows the ample luggage carrier inside the new 7-h.p. Jowett.

The most expensive car in the show, the 45 h.p. Duesenberg straight eight.

A feature of the Duesenberg chassis is this automatic oil-feeder, which shows a green light on the dashboard when all is well and a red light when anything goes wrong. This apparatus looks after the oil-feed every seventy or eighty miles.

The Motor Show which opens at Olympia to-day will prove to be the best and brightest ever held in Britain or in any other country. It comprises one million pounds' worth of cars, which are fitted with many interesting improvements. Never before has Olympia housed such magnificent stands and decorations.

"DAILY MIRROR" ZIG-ZAG PUZZLE: £500 PRIZE

£10,000 ACCIDENT INSURANCE

DailyMirror

THE DAILY PICTURE PAPER WITH THE LARGEST NET SALE

SPECIAL EDITION

No. 8,090 | Registered at the G.P.O as a Newspaper | MONDAY, OCTOBER 21, 1929 | One Penny

FIRE DESTROYS WEMBLEY TALKIE STUDIOS

Looking down into wrecked and smouldering buildings comprised in the old Wembley Garden Club, after a fire which destroyed sound film studios yesterday.

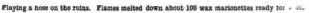

Playing a hose on the ruins. Flames melted down about 100 wax marionettes ready for a film.

Examining what remains of a sound-production machine. Valuable apparatus was in burned-out experimental rooms.

A furious blaze broke out early yesterday in the Wembley Exhibition grounds and destroyed two sound film studios of British Talking Pictures, Ltd., together with adjoining rooms and offices. Unexposed films exploded, but exposed films were safely removed from a special vault. Firemen, who were delayed by fog, succeeded in preventing the flames from spreading to new and finely equipped studios that were ready for their opening next month. See also page 28.—(" Daily Mirror " photographs.)

THE DAILY MIRROR, Tuesday, October 22, 1929.

MANY INSURANCE CLAIMS PAID: REGISTER NOW

LAUGH DAILY WITH THE PATER

DailyMirror

THE DAILY PICTURE PAPER WITH THE LARGEST NET SALE

No. 8,091 — Registered at the G.P.O. as a Newspaper. — TUESDAY, OCTOBER 22, 1929 — One Penny

£500 ZIG-ZAG PUZZLE

169 MAKE RECORD FLIGHT IN GIANT 'PLANE

The German flying-ship Do. X., the largest in the world, in the air.

BABY'S DEATH

The Hon. Mrs. Francis Erskine, whose infant son was found suffocated at his parents' London home yesterday. She is the wife of the Earl of Mar and Kellie's second son.

AN OPERATION

M. Poincaré, who resigned the French Premiership owing to ill-health, underwent a second operation in Paris yesterday. A bulletin states that it was done " under very good conditions."

Dr. Dornier, the designer of the Do. X., which carried 150 passengers and a crew of nineteen in an epoch-making flight on Lake Constance yesterday. Right, a crowd of 169 people, illustrating the number on board the wonder-'plane. The feat is easily a record for any flying craft, either heavier or lighter than air. The Do. X. was up for fifty minutes. She will make long-distance flights in the spring as a preliminary to an attempt to cross the Atlantic. It is believed that she could float for weeks, if necessary.

THE DAILY MIRROR, Thursday, October 24, 1929.

BRILLIANT NEW SERIAL BEGINS NEXT MONDAY

£10,000 ACCIDENT INSURANCE

Daily Mirror

THE DAILY PICTURE ● PAPER WITH THE LARGEST NET SALE

SPECIAL EDITION

No. 8,093 | Registered at the G.P.O. as a Newspaper. | THURSDAY, OCTOBER 24, 1929 | One Penny

CANADIAN'S LONE ATLANTIC FLIGHT ATTEMPT

Mr. U. F. Diteman in the cockpit of the Golden Hind, in which he started from St. Johns, Newfoundland, on Tuesday on an attempt to emulate Colonel Lindbergh.

Viewing the bold airman's machine at its starting-point. He is a cattle rancher of Billings, Montana, and claims descent from Sir Francis Drake.

Orders were given for Croydon Aerodrome to be lit up throughout the night for Mr. Diteman. Anxiety for his safety was felt as he was long overdue. The Golden Hind started with 165 gallons of petrol, which allowed for a twenty-five hours' flight. If all had gone well, he should have crossed the Irish coast yesterday morning and reached Croydon at 1 p.m. A Queenstown weather report described coastal visibility as poor owing to mist and light rain.—(Special "Daily Mirror" photographs.)

"JASMINE—TAKE CARE!" BEGINS ON MONDAY

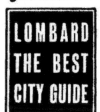

LOMBARD THE BEST CITY GUIDE

DailyMirror

THE DAILY PICTURE PAPER WITH THE LARGEST NET SALE

SPECIAL EDITION

No. 8,094 — Registered at the G.P.O. as a Newspaper. — FRIDAY, OCTOBER 25, 1929 — One Penny

MAN WHO SHOT AT ITALIAN PRINCE

The arrest of Fernando di Rosa after he shot at Prince Umberto, the young Crown Prince of Italy, with a revolver in Brussels yesterday. The attempt took place at the Tomb of the Unknown Soldier a few hours after the announcement of the Prince's betrothal to Princess Marie Jose, daughter of King Albert. The Prince remained completely calm and carried out the programme arranged. The arrest of his assailant, an Italian law student in Paris, was accomplished only after a fierce struggle, in which about ten policemen took part. Princess Marie Jose had great difficulty in keeping her composure when told the news. See also pages 14 and 15.

THE DAILY MIRROR, Tuesday, October 29, 1929.

MANY INSURANCE CLAIMS PAID: REGISTER NOW

BEGIN OUR NEW SERIAL TO-DAY

DailyMirror

THE DAILY PICTURE PAPER WITH THE LARGEST NET SALE

No. 8,097 | Registered at the G.P.O. as a Newspaper. | TUESDAY, OCTOBER 29, 1929 | One Penny

£100 CROSSWORD PUZZLE

HOUNDS AT VISCOUNTESS'S WEDDING

A huntsman in charge of hounds of the Grafton Hunt toasting Major Gavin Hume-Gore, of the Gordon Highlanders, and his bride, Viscountess Ipswich, after their marriage at Whittlebury, Northants, yesterday. The bride has hunted since she was fifteen. Also 'n the picture are her daughters (bareheaded), the Hon. Margaret Jane and the Hon. Mary Rose FitzRoy, who sang in the choir of girls at the ceremony, and Miss Jean Hume-Gore, daughter of the bridegroom. Viscount Ipswich, who is fifteen and heir to the Dukedom of Grafton, gave his mother away. Viscountess Ipswich's former husband was killed in a flying accident in 1918. See also page 28.—("Daily Mirror.")

RAMBLER COMPLETES THE "AUTUMN DOUBLE"

£500 PICTURE PUZZLE WEEKLY

DailyMirror

THE DAILY PICTURE PAPER WITH THE LARGEST NET SALE

BEST FAMILY INSURANCE

No. 8,099   Registered at the G.P.O. as a Newspaper.   THURSDAY, OCTOBER 31, 1929   One Penny

LADY ZIA WERNHER'S CAMBRIDGESHIRE WIN

Double Life, ridden by J. Dines, its jockey yesterday.

The finish of the Cambridgeshire takes, won yesterday by Double Life.

A picture taken at the same instant as the one above, but from the opposite side of the course. A neck separated first and second.   Lady Zia Wernher.

Lady Zia Wernher, a daughter of the Grand Duke Michael of Russia, won the Cambridgeshire Stakes yesterday with Double Life, which beat Vatout and Palais Royal II., last year's winner. Double Life, which was No. 13 on the race card and was backed at 20-1, was bred by J. Dines, its jockey yesterday, and sold as a yearling to Lady Zia Wernher for 600 guineas. It was only in the last strides of a desperate finish that it got ahead in a huge field of thirty-six.

THE DAILY MIRROR, Monday, November 4, 1929.

CRITICAL WEEK FOR THE GOVERNMENT: SEE P. 3

FILM NOTES TO-DAY

DailyMirror
THE DAILY PICTURE PAPER WITH THE LARGEST NET SALE

No. 8,102 | Registered at the G.P.O. as a Newspaper | MONDAY, NOVEMBER 4, 1929 | One Penny

NEW £500 PICTURE PUZZLE

LEADING FIGURES IN THE INDIA STATUS MOVE

The Simon Commission seated in session at the Law Courts. (A to B) Hon. E. Cadogan, Major Attlee, Lord Burnham, Lord Strathcona, Colonel Lane-Fox, Mr. Vernon Hartshorn and Sir John Simon (chairman). It has been revealed that they were not consulted before the Viceroy made his statement regarding Dominion status for India.

Lord Reading, who will raise the question of India in the House of Lords to-morrow.

Mr. Stanley Baldwin, whose personal statement regarding India will be on Thursday.

Mr. Ramsay MacDonald, who will no doubt take an active part in this week's exciting events.

Captain Wedgwood-Benn, Secretary for India, will also be prominent in the India debate.

Lord Irwin, Viceroy of India, whose declaration on Dominion status started the agitation.

Among the subjects which will cause anxiety to the Government this week is that of India. In the House of Lords to-morrow Lord Reading, a former Viceroy, will ask for reasons for the "extraordinary course" of making the Irwin declaration without reference to the Simon Commission. The matter will be further debated in the House of Commons on Thursday. The questions of unemployment and relations with Russia will also cause considerable political excitement.

CONVERSION LOAN: STOCK EXCHANGE INDIGNANT

GRAMOPHONE NOTES TO-DAY

DailyMirror

THE DAILY PICTURE PAPER WITH THE LARGEST NET SALE

No. 8,105 Registered at the G.P.O. as a Newspaper. THURSDAY, NOVEMBER 7, 1929 One Penny

LOMBARD THE BEST CITY GUIDE

SIX KILLED IN CRASH OF AN AIR LINER

The ill-fated German all-metal and triple-engined air liner D 903 in flight from Croydon.

Bruno Rodschinka, chief pilot, killed.

Mr. D. L. Jones, a dead passenger.

Lt.-Comdr. Glen Kidston, slightly burned.

Prince von Schaumberg-Lippe, severely burned.

Wreckage of the German air liner which crashed in flames near Marden Park, Surrey, yesterday, with the loss of six lives, those of three passengers and three of the crew. The machine was on a flight to Amsterdam and Berlin and struck trees soon after leaving Croydon. Lieutenant-Commander Glen Kidston, the famous racing motorist, who had just left a sick bed to go to Berlin on business, had a marvellous escape, and within a few hours with his head in bandages was in the air again at Croydon " to test his flying nerve." Prince Eugen Schaumberg-Lippe, the second pilot, escaped from the machine with clothes ablaze. See also pages 14 and 15.—(" Daily Mirror " photograph.)

V.C. NUMBER TO-MORROW: SPECIAL PHOTOGRAPHS

RADIO GOSSIP TO-DAY

DailyMirror

THE DAILY PICTURE PAPER WITH THE LARGEST NET SALE

No. 8,106 | Registered at the G.P.O. as a Newspaper. | FRIDAY, NOVEMBER 8, 1929 | One Penny

BEST FAMILY INSURANCE

'PLANE FIRES HOUSES AFTER AIR COLLISION

Firemen playing a hose on the burning houses.

The houses in Ross-road after the blaze, and remains of a 'plane.

Wreckage of one of the 'planes in Tharp-road, and damaged shed.

Following a collision between two R.A.F. single-seater 'planes at a height of about a mile over Wallington, Surrey, yesterday, the pilots, Flying Officer E. S. Collins and Flight Sergeant White, used their parachutes and safely came down. One of the machines crashed on to the roof of a house and set it alight. It then fell, a mass of flames, into the garden, and the adjacent house was also damaged. The other 'plane crashed on to a garden shed. No one was hurt.

ARMISTICE DAY CEREMONIES: FULL DETAILS

BUY A POPPY

TO-DAY

Daily Mirror

THE DAILY PICTURE PAPER WITH THE LARGEST NET SALE

No. 8,108 Registered at the G.P.O. as a Newspaper. MONDAY, NOVEMBER 11, 1929 One Penny

BUY A POPPY

TO-DAY

TO-DAY'S GREAT REMEMBRANCE

One of the many British war cemeteries scattered near former battlefields, and, below, infantry attacking enemy entrenchments—pictures that typify the nation's thought to-day, the eleventh anniversary of the Armistice, when the whole Empire joins in solemn homage to the million British dead of the Great War. The bitterness of conflict has gone, but our gratitude to those who gave their whole remains. The Prince of Wales will represent the King at the service at the Cenotaph, where 319 V.C.s will be present,

THE DAILY MIRROR. Friday, November 15, 1929.

£500 ZIG-ZAG PUZZLE ON SALE TO-MORROW

RADIO GOSSIP TO-DAY

DailyMirror

THE DAILY PICTURE PAPER WITH THE LARGEST NET SALE

No. 8,112   Registered at the G.P.O. as a Newspaper.   FRIDAY, NOVEMBER 15, 1929   One Penny

BEST FAMILY INSURANCE

EARLY FORETASTE OF WINTER

MAJOR-GENERAL'S QUIET WEDDING

Walking along a snow-covered path between Whaley Bridge and Buxton during the first fall of snow in the Peak this winter.

Major-General Simpson and his bride, Miss Mary Cochrane, daughter of the late Rev. T. Cochrane, formerly rector of Stapleford Abbots, Essex, leaving St. Michael's, Chester-square, yesterday.

Players of the Newcastle Caledonian Curling Club who yesterday took part in the first match of the season on a splendid sheet of ice at Ryton, Durham.—(By "Daily Mirror" photo-telephony.)

Deep snow on a main road in Yorkshire. For a stretch of over four miles about nine inches of snow lay on the ground.

The snow which was seen in the Lake District early this week was followed by falls farther south, but forecasts last night did not anticipate any further fall, although rather cold weather with night frosts inland is to be expected to-day. In some places where the snow has lain road traffic has been impeded.

OUR £500 ZIG-ZAG PUZZLE ON SALE TO-DAY

LAUGH DAILY WITH THE PATER

DailyMirror

THE DAILY PICTURE PAPER WITH THE LARGEST NET SALE

LOMBARD THE BEST CITY GUIDE

No. 8,113 — Registered at the G.P.O. as a Newspaper. — SATURDAY, NOVEMBER 16, 1929 — One Penny

£500 ZIG-ZAG PUZZLE

NEW HEALTH EXHIBITS

Examples of reformed dresses at the New Health Society's Exhibition, which was opened at the Royal Horticultural Hall, Westminster, yesterday. In the centre is Gibb McLaughlan, film actor. The exhibition will remain open until Friday.—("Daily Mirror.")

YACHTSWOMEN'S £35 FINE

A PEER'S DEATH

The "Daily Mirror" zig-zag puzzle, which is on sale to-day at all bookstalls. A prize of £500 is offered for the correct arrangement of the pieces, an arrangement known only to the Editor of the "Daily Mirror." Already a quarter of a million copies of this fascinating puzzle, a few pieces of which are omitted from the photograph, have been disposed of. Full details will be found on page 3.

Miss Susan Ryder, and (inset) Miss Marjorie Bagot, the yachtswomen upon whom a combined fine of £35 16s. 4d. was imposed at Dover yesterday on a charge of importing goods with intent to avoid payment of duty.

Lord Blythswood, who died at Blythswood House, Renfrew, aged fifty-nine. He was a friend of the Royal Family and Deputy-Lieutenant of Glasgow, Lanark, Glamorgan, Renfrew.

MANY INSURANCE CLAIMS PAID: REGISTER NOW

FREE XMAS HAMPERS

Daily Mirror

THE DAILY PICTURE PAPER WITH THE LARGEST NET SALE

No. 8,115   Registered at the G.P.O. as a Newspaper.   TUESDAY, NOVEMBER 19, 1929   One Penny

GET YOUR ZIG-ZAG TO-DAY

CARNERA BEATS STRIBLING ON A FOUL

Primo Carnera, the Italian boxing giant, on the boards after the foul blow which disqualified Young Stribling in their big fight last night.

Baby Stribling watching his father's fight.

The two boxers sparring for an opening.

The Prince of Wales at the ringside.

The Carnera-Stribling fight, which has aroused such intense interest, ended at the Albert Hall last night in the fourth round, after Stribling had delivered a low blow which put his giant opponent on the boards. Until then he had boxed like a winner and had even in the previous round with a blow to the jaw lifted Carnera, some 6½st. heavier than himself, off his feet. He always seemed able to dodge Carnera's leads, and was cleverer in the clinches. Other pictures are on page 28.

THE DAILY MIRROR, Thursday November 21, 1929.

£500 FOR ZIG-ZAG PUZZLE SOLUTION: SEE PAGE 4

GRAMOPHONE
ARTICLE
TO-DAY

DailyMirror

THE DAILY PICTURE PAPER WITH THE LARGEST NET SALE

BEST
FAMILY
INSURANCE

No. 8,117   Registered at the G.P.O. as a Newspaper.   THURSDAY, NOVEMBER 21, 1929   One Penny

FLOODS WHICH FOLLOWED TORRENTIAL RAIN

Delivery of food and drink to imprisoned residents of Aberdulais, Glamorgan.

Water waist-high in the main street of Porth. The police station and the Post Office were flooded.

Porth Railway Station. Part of the track was swept away near here.

The torrential rain in South Wales flooded many towns and left thousands of acres of land and many roads under water. Eighty families were cut off at Pontypridd, and at Llansamlet people forced from their homes spent the night in the church hall. The bursting of a dam wall near Neath caused great damage. See also page 12.

DR. KNOWLES FREE—HOAX ON CROWD

The car in which Mrs. Ashby, Dr. Benjamin Knowles's sister, arrived at Maidstone Prison yesterday leaving the main gates. Dr. Knowles left through the Assize Court, and the crowd outside the prison cheered the wrong car.

THE DAILY MIRROR. Wednesday, November 27, 1929.

WONDER HOUSE: FIRST PICTURES TO-MORROW

£500 FOR A ZIG-ZAG SOLUTION

Daily Mirror

THE DAILY PICTURE PAPER WITH THE LARGEST NET SALE

No. 8,122   Registered at the G.P.O. as a Newspaper.   WEDNESDAY, NOVEMBER 27, 1929   One Penny

BEST FAMILY INSURANCE

EIGHT LIVES LOST IN LONDON SHIP

Heavy seas battering the London steamer Molesey, the vessel for which the B.B.C. broadcast an SOS to ships in the vicinity, after she had gone on the rocks near Wooltack Point, Pembrokeshire, yesterday, eight lives, those of the chief officer's wife and seven members of the crew, being lost in the wreck. For eighteen hours, which included the night, those on board had an experience of horror while the vessel was swept with such huge seas that no lifeboat could approach. Yesterday morning the Milford Haven lifeboat succeeded in reaching the wreck and in taking off twenty-eight persons, including two women. The picture below shows some of these at Milford Haven.

MAYFAIR WOMAN ARRESTED BY MISTAKE

FREE XMAS HAMPERS

DailyMirror

THE DAILY PICTURE PAPER WITH THE LARGEST NET SALE

No. 8,123   Registered at the G.P.O. as a Newspaper.   THURSDAY, NOVEMBER 28, 1929   One Penny

£500 ZIG-ZAG PUZZLE

THE PETS' WONDER HOUSE—FIRST PICTURES

The wonderful "model" house for Pip, Squeak and Wilfred to be exhibited at the Grafton Galleries from December 19. This "ancestral home" of the famous "Daily Mirror" pets is 7ft. 6in. in height and has twelve rooms, and it has been designed by Mr. Maxwell Ayrton, F.R.I.B.A. This picture and the others on pages 12 and 13 are the first of the model to be published and they give a complete idea of an artistic and enchanting creation which will enthrall every member of the great Gugnunc family.

116

"PUBLIC CONFIDENCE SERIOUSLY SHAKEN": P.18

£500 FOR A ZIG-ZAG SOLUTION

DailyMirror

THE DAILY PICTURE PAPER WITH THE LARGEST NET SALE

100 FREE XMAS HAMPERS WEEKLY

No. 8,126 | Registered at the G.P.O. as a Newspaper. | MONDAY, DECEMBER 2, 1929 | One Penny

FRANCE HONOURS CLEMENCEAU'S MEMORY

President Doumergue (X) and the French Cabinet during the one minute's silence in memory of M. Clemenceau at the Tomb of the Unknown Soldier, Paris.

Girls from Alsace and Lorraine in traditional dress at the head of a delegation from the regained provinces. Representatives of all ex-Service men's organisations were present at the Arc de Triomphe for the official tribute at the Tomb of the Unknown Soldier to France's Grand Old Man, who did so much to save his country.— ("Daily Mirror" photographs.)

KING AND QUEEN OF DENMARK MET BY THE PRINCE

The Prince of Wales with the King and Queen of Denmark, whom he met on their arrival in London last night. The motor-ship in which the visitors travelled went ashore in a fog shortly after leaving Esbjerg and was refloated several hours later.—("Daily Mirror.")

117

BEGIN OUR BRILLIANT NEW SERIAL TO-DAY

£500 FOR A ZIG-ZAG SOLUTION

DailyMirror

THE DAILY PICTURE PAPER WITH THE LARGEST NET SALE

SPECIAL EDITION

No. 8,130   Registered at the G.P.O. as a Newspaper.   FRIDAY, DECEMBER 6, 1929   One Penny

HAVOC OF THE GREAT 94-MILE PER HOUR GALE

The boundary wall of the Great Western Railway blown down at the junction of Royal Oak Bridge and Harrow-road.

Hole made in a roof by a fallen chimney at Dartmouth. Two children were injured and taken to hospital.

A train running through flood water at Clock House Station, near Beckenham, Kent, where the River Ravensbourne overflowed its banks owing to the heavy rainfall and gale. The electric service was interrupted.

Trying to look like a lighthouse—traffic signal on flooded Kingston by-pass road.

Uprooted tree lying across a road at Pinhoe, near Exeter.

Extensive damage was done in many places by the great gale which swept Southern England and Wales during the early hours of yesterday. The wind at many points reached a velocity of ninety-four miles per hour. There were high seas in the English Channel and some of the Continental boat services were suspended. See also pages 16 and 17.

118

MANY INSURANCE CLAIMS PAID: REGISTER NOW

FIRST
WAR
STORIES
TO-DAY

DailyMirror

THE DAILY PICTURE PAPER WITH THE LARGEST NET SALE

No. 8,133   Registered at the G.P.O. as a Newspaper.   TUESDAY, DECEMBER 10, 1929   One Penny

£1,000
MUST-BE-WON
ZIG-ZAG
PRIZE

GRAVE PERIL FROM EVER RISING THAMES

Road and river traffic side by side at the same level—at Boulter's Lock.

The greatly swollen Thames pouring last night over Teddington Weir, where the river level is carefully watched for signs of danger.

A riverside building and two boathouses flooded up to the eaves at Maidenhead.

With forecasts of more storms over the South of England and the prospect of spring tides, the greatest anxiety is felt as to the possibility of further severe flooding by the Thames. Lord Desborough announced yesterday that during the last ten weeks the nor-mal rainfall of six winter months had fallen in the Thames Valley. He said that were the rain to stop at once the river would continue to rise for two or three days. Other flood pictures will be found on page 15.

GUINEAS FOR WAR TALES: SEND YOURS TO-DAY

£1,000 ZIG-ZAG PUZZLE

DailyMirror

THE DAILY PICTURE PAPER WITH THE LARGEST NET SALE

HELP THE GUGNUNC XMAS FUND

No. 8,135 — Registered at the G.P.O. as a Newspaper. — THURSDAY, DECEMBER 12, 1929 — One Penny

LONG TUBE HOLD-UPS

Windows damaged at Lots-road power station, Chelsea, yesterday, when the current failed during the morning rush hours and trains on the District Railway and tubes and London United Tramways were twice held up for a considerable period.

BANKER'S MARRIAGE

Sir Eric Hambro and his bride, Mrs. Elger, leaving Princes-row register office after their marriage yesterday. Sir Eric is chairman of Hambro's Bank and sub-governor of the Royal Exchange Assurance Company.

"HUSH HUSH" ENGINE FOR HIGH SPEEDS—PRINCIPLES NEW TO BRITISH RAILWAYS

A giant engine secretly built at Darlington for the London and North-Eastern Railway. It embodies principles of boiler construction which are new to British railways and is specially designed for high speed traffic on the East Coast route. It has been constructed to the design of Mr. H. N. Gresley, the chief mechanical engineer of the railway.

PIP & SQUEAK'S HOUSE ON SHOW NEXT WEEK See page 2

HELP THE GUGNUNC XMAS FUND

DailyMirror

THE DAILY PICTURE PAPER WITH THE LARGEST NET SALE

No. 8,137   Registered at the G.P.O. as a Newspaper.   SATURDAY, DECEMBER 14, 1929   One Penny

£1,000 ZIG-ZAG PUZZLE

ATTACKED IN FOILED RAID

Mr. W. T. Thorpe, attacked when a bag containing £700 was taken by bandits from cashiers in a City office. Five men were detained. The money was recovered.

BACK FROM U.S.

Miss Valerie French, granddaughter of the late Earl of Ypres, back from America. Asked regarding her reported re-engagement to a former fiancé she said, "There is no engagement."

LAST BRITISH TROOPS FROM RHINE

The last British troops to evacuate the Rhineland arriving at Dover on the Marie-Jose from Ostend yesterday. Inset, Lieutenant-General Sir William Thwaites, who was Commander-in-Chief of the British Army of Occupation, photographed at Victoria Station with his wife. At Ostend the British officers had exchanged toasts with a delegation of Belgian officers on board.

FORTIFYING THE THAMES FOR LONDON'S DANGER DAYS

Reinforcing with sandbags the Thames Embankment at Grosvenor-road last night. London's danger time from high tides will begin on Monday, when the moon is full, and will last until Thursday. See page 12.

HELPING DISMISSED WORKERS

Lady Houston, who has offered to pay until over the New Year the wages of about 115 Hull men who volunteered for tramway work during the general strike and whom the Town Council, with a Socialist majority, has now decided to dismiss.

PETS' WONDER HOUSE ON VIEW THIS WEEK. P. 2

100 FREE HAMPERS

DailyMirror

THE DAILY PICTURE PAPER WITH THE LARGEST NET SALE

SPECIAL EDITION

No. 8,138   Registered at the G.P.O. as a Newspaper.   MONDAY, DECEMBER 16, 1929   One Penny

THREAT OF HIGH TIDE FLOODS IN LONDON

Thames water lapping over the wharf just below Vauxhall Bridge at high tide yesterday afternoon. During the next few days the high tides will be the most critical in the flood areas of London, and anxious watch in consequence is being kept on the Thames.

THE INFLUENZA GERM AT LAST TO BE CONQUERED?

Dr. David Thomson, who, with his brother, Dr. R. Thomson, has been making determined efforts in London to isolate the influenza germ. He hopes that recent experiments, some carried out by Dr. S. Falk, of Chicago, will prove that a germ he has isolated is the one responsible, in which case a preventive vaccine could be produced.

PARIS HONOURS LADY HAIG

Lady Haig in Paris, where she went to rekindle the flame at the Tomb of the French Unknown Soldier. With her is M. Scapini (tallest), president of the War Blind.

MANY INSURANCE CLAIMS PAID: REGISTER NOW

GUINEAS FOR WAR TALES AND DRAWINGS

DailyMirror
THE DAILY PICTURE ● PAPER WITH THE LARGEST NET SALE

No. 8,139 — Registered at the G.P.O. as a Newspaper. — TUESDAY, DECEMBER 17, 1929 — One Penny

£100 CROSSWORD PUZZLE

R 100's FINE MAIDEN FLIGHT

The 700ft. long airship R 100 reflected in a flooded field when moored to the mast at Cardington, Bedfordshire, yesterday, after her maiden flight from Howden, Yorkshire. The journey of 140 miles took two hours and the airship was in the air for six hours. Inset, Commander Sir Dennistoun Burney (smoking), the designer, and Major Scott, who was in command. See also pages 12 and 13.

DISCLOSURES IN THE HATRY CASE

Sir Gilbert Garnsey (bareheaded), the accountant, who gave evidence at the Guildhall yesterday, and Clarence Hatry, who with three associates, was committed for trial. Sir Gilbert estimated the deficiencies in Hatry companies at £13,500,000. Hatry made a dramatic speech.

MARRIAGE OF A BARONET

Sir Anthony Lindsay-Hogg and his bride, Miss Frances Doble, the actress, leaving St. Margaret's, Westminster.

A page, Archie Kidston, son of Lieutenant-Commander Glen Kidston, the motorist, being carried from the church by his mother.—("Daily Mirror" photographs.)

123

THE QUEEN VISITS MIRROR GRANGE: SEE P. 2

ZIG-ZAG
THE BEST
XMAS
GAME

DailyMirror

THE DAILY PICTURE PAPER WITH THE LARGEST NET SALE

No. 8,141   Registered at the G.P.O. as a Newspaper.   THURSDAY, DECEMBER 19, 1929   One Penny

HELP THE
GUGNUNC
FUND

MIRROR GRANGE TO BE ON VIEW TO-DAY

Mirror Grange, the Pets' new miniature home at the top of a cliff.

H.M. the Queen, who paid a private visit to the model house yesterday.

Mr. Maxwell Ayrton, F.R.I.B.A., who is the designer of Mirror Grange.

Mr. George Sheringham has been Mr. Ayrton's confrere throughout the construction of the model.

Miniature furniture being made for this wonderful model of a country home.

The dining-room disclosed. All the rooms can be seen similarly.

The Queen paid a visit yesterday to Grafton Galleries, Bond-street, to see Mirror Grange, the ancestral home of Pip, Squeak and Wilfred, which will be opened to view by the general public at four o'clock to-day. The Queen appeared to be delighted with all she saw. The house will be visited by thousands of Gugnuncs and other home-lovers who will flock to see the Pets' model home during the next few weeks, and our advice to all is "Get there early." Mr. George Sheringham (whose portrait appears above) has been very largely responsible for the interior decoration and furnishing, and the colouring of the model was executed on his advice. See also page 12.

HOUSE COLLAPSE IN GREAT GALE: TWO DEAD

ZIG-ZAG
CLOSING
DATE

DailyMirror

THE DAILY PICTURE PAPER WITH THE LARGEST NET SALE

No. 8,148 Registered at the G.P.O. as a Newspaper. MONDAY, DECEMBER 30, 1929 One Penny

150
FREE
HAMPERS

BRITAIN AGAIN IN GRIP OF GALE AND FLOOD

Huge seas pounding against the front and breaking into great clouds of spray at Hastings, where the full force of yesterday's gale was felt.

A house in Harriet-street, Manchester, which collapsed yesterday. Two persons were killed.

A large tree which was blown down in Hyde Park and snapped in two.

An enormous wave breaking at Scarborough yesterday. It just missed the car.

During the height of yesterday's great gale, in which both north and south suffered, a house collapsed at Manchester, killing Mrs. Margaret Sullivan and her daughter Winifred. Four other children were in the house and of these two girls were rescued by men who put a ladder against an upper window. A boy and a girl were found slightly injured among the debris. Terrible weather was experienced along the coasts and in Kent lifeboats were busy. See also pages 12 and 13.

125

STILL TIME TO SOLVE £1,000 ZIG-ZAG PUZZLE

MORE INSURANCE CLAIMS PAID

DailyMirror

THE DAILY PICTURE PAPER WITH THE LARGEST NET SALE

No. 8,149   Registered at the G.P.O. as a Newspaper.   TUESDAY, DECEMBER 31, 1929   One Penny

£100 CROSSWORD PUZZLE

THREE KILLED IN BLAZING CAR COLLISION

Mr. William Wild, who was killed.

Flight-Lieutenant J. F. Lawson, who was killed.

Mr. A. Wild, injured.

Remains of the car and motor-cycle which were in collision and caught fire at Wimbledon Common.

MYSTERY OF THE STORM—HAS AN UNKNOWN SHIP FOUNDERED?

Driftwood and bales of crepe rubber at the base of the Falling Sands, near Beachy Head, yesterday. Various kinds of cargo have been found and it is feared that a vessel, as yet unknown, has sunk.

Mrs. J. F. Lawson, who with Mr. W. A. F. Wild was also killed. Flight-Lieutenant and Mrs. Lawson were in the car and Mr. Wild was driving the motor-cycle. Mr. A. R. Wild, brother of the motor-cycle driver, was thrown from the pillion and badly injured.

Printed in Great Britain
by Amazon

36256493R00072